THE WRITING ART
Authorship as Experienced and Expressed by the Great Writers

THE WRITING ART
AUTHORSHIP AS EXPERIENCED AND
EXPRESSED BY THE GREAT WRITERS

An Anthology

SELECTED BY
BERTHA W. SMITH
AND
VIRGINIA C. LINCOLN
Editors of The Writer

BOSTON AND NEW YORK
HOUGHTON MIFFLIN COMPANY
The Riverside Press Cambridge
1931

COPYRIGHT, 1931, BY BERTHA W. SMITH AND VIRGINIA C. LINCOLN

ALL RIGHTS RESERVED

The Riverside Press
CAMBRIDGE · MASSACHUSETTS
PRINTED IN THE U.S.A.

ACKNOWLEDGMENT

THE editors gratefully acknowledge the courtesy of permission accorded for the inclusion of copyrighted material from the following sources: To George Allen and Unwin, Ltd., for quotations from 'Zones of the Spirit: A Book of Thoughts,' by August Strindberg, and 'Turgeniev, and His French Circle,' edited by E. Halperine-Kaminsky: translated by Ethel M. Arnold; to Bobbs-Merrill Company, for quotations from 'Letters from Joseph Conrad,' edited by Edward Garnett; to Thomas Y. Crowell Company, for quotations from 'Eminent Authors of the Nineteenth Century,' by Georg Brandes; to Doubleday, Doran and Company, for quotations from 'O. Henry,' by C. Alphonso Smith, and 'Two Prefaces,' by Walt Whitman; to Duffield and Green, for quotations from 'Letters of Henrik Ibsen,' translated by John Nilsen Laurvik and Mary Morison Fox; to E. P. Dutton and Company, for quotations from 'Critical Essays,' by Charles Lamb, and 'Gogol,' by Janko Lavrin; to T. N. Foulis Company, for quotations from 'The Complete Works of Friedrich Nietzsche,' edited by Oscar Levy; to Freemantle and Company, for quotations from 'The Memoirs of François René Vicomte de Chateaubriand,' translated by Alexander Teixeira de Mattos; to Harper and Brothers, for quotations from 'Postscripts,' by O. Henry, 'Literature and

Life,' by William Dean Howells, and 'Mark Twain's Autobiography,' Introduction by Albert Bigelow Paine; to Harvard University Press, for quotations from 'Essays of Montaigne,' translated by George B. Ives; to Hodder and Stoughton, for quotations from 'The Brontës, Life and Letters,' by Clement Shorter; to Houghton Mifflin Company, for quotations from 'The Heart of Burroughs's Journals,' edited by Clara Barrus, 'The Life and Letters of Emily Dickinson,' by her niece, Martha Dickinson Bianchi, 'Letters and Social Aims,' by Ralph Waldo Emerson, 'Journals of Ralph Waldo Emerson,' edited by Edward Waldo Emerson and Waldo Emerson Forbes, Vol. X, 'The Heart of Hawthorne's Journals,' edited by Newton Arvin, 'The Autocrat of the Breakfast Table,' by Oliver Wendell Holmes, 'Life of Henry Wadsworth Longfellow,' by Samuel Longfellow, 'Among My Books,' by James Russell Lowell, 'Autumn, from the Journal of Henry D. Thoreau,' edited by H. G. O. Blake, 'Familiar Letters of Henry David Thoreau,' edited by F. B. Sanborn, and 'Letters of George Sand,' translated by Veronica Lucas; to Mildred Howells and John Mead Howells, for quotations from 'Literature and Life,' by William Dean Howells; to Little, Brown and Company, for quotations from 'The Letters of William James,' edited by his son, Henry James, 'Honoré de Balzac,' translated by Katharine Prescott Wormeley, and 'The Æsthetic Letters, Essays, and the Philosophical Letters of Schiller,' translated by J. Weiss; to The Macmillan

ACKNOWLEDGMENT vii

Company, for quotations from 'The Later Years of Thomas Hardy,' by Florence Emily Hardy, 'Letters of Fyodor Michailovitch Dostoevsky,' translated by Ethel Colburn Mayne, 'An Introduction to the Prose and Poetical Works of John Milton,' by Hiram Corson, 'Correspondence between Goethe and Carlyle,' edited by Charles Eliot Norton; to The Nonesuch Press, Ltd., for quotations from 'Poetry and Prose of William Blake,' edited by Geoffrey Keynes; to Mary Riley Payne, Elizabeth E. Miesse, and Edmund H. Eitel, for quotations from 'The Letters of James Whitcomb Riley,' edited by William Lyon Phelps; to G. P. Putnam's Sons, for quotations from 'Readings from Washington Irving,' selected from 'The Sketch-Book' and 'The Alhambra,' and quotations from 'Voltaire in His Letters,' by S. G. Tallentyre; to Charles Scribner's Sons, for quotations from 'Essays of Travel and in the Art of Writing,' by Robert Louis Stevenson, 'Boswell's Life of Johnson,' edited by Charles Grosvenor Osgood, 'An Essay on Comedy,' by George Meredith, and 'Essays by William Hazlitt,' edited by Percy Van Dyke Shelly; also selections from Modern Student's Library (Addison and Steele).

CONTENTS

AMERICAN WRITERS

HENRY WARD BEECHER (1813–1887)	1
JOHN BURROUGHS (1837–1921)	2
EMILY DICKINSON (1830–1886)	7
RALPH WALDO EMERSON (1803–1882)	12
BENJAMIN FRANKLIN (1706–1790)	15
NATHANIEL HAWTHORNE (1804–1864)	17
O. HENRY (WILLIAM SYDNEY PORTER) (1862–1910)	20
OLIVER WENDELL HOLMES (1809–1894)	24
WILLIAM DEAN HOWELLS (1837–1920)	27
WASHINGTON IRVING (1783–1859)	35
WILLIAM JAMES (1842–1910)	37
HENRY WADSWORTH LONGFELLOW (1807–1882)	41
JAMES RUSSELL LOWELL (1819–1891)	45
JAMES WHITCOMB RILEY (1853–1916)	55
HENRY D. THOREAU (1817–1862)	60
MARK TWAIN (SAMUEL LANGHORNE CLEMENS) (1835–1910)	63
WALT WHITMAN (1819–1892)	67

BRITISH WRITERS

JOSEPH ADDISON (1672–1719)	70
WILLIAM BLAKE (1757–1827)	73
JAMES BOSWELL (1740–1795)	75
CHARLOTTE BRONTË (1816–1855)	78

CONTENTS

EMILY BRONTË (1818–1848)	79
ELIZABETH BARRETT BROWNING (1806–1861)	81
ROBERT BURNS (1759–1796)	86
SAMUEL BUTLER (1612–1680)	88
LORD BYRON (1788–1824)	92
SAMUEL TAYLOR COLERIDGE (1772–1834)	102
JOSEPH CONRAD (1857–1924)	104
CHARLES DICKENS (1812–1870)	109
BENJAMIN DISRAELI (1804–1881)	111
THOMAS HARDY (1840–1928)	113
WILLIAM HAZLITT (1778–1830)	116
LEIGH HUNT (1784–1859)	121
SAMUEL JOHNSON (1709–1784)	124
JOHN KEATS (1795–1821)	125
CHARLES LAMB (1775–1834)	127
THOMAS BABINGTON MACAULAY (1800–1859)	129
GEORGE MEREDITH (1828–1909)	130
JOHN MILTON (1608–1674)	132
JOHN HENRY CARDINAL NEWMAN (1801–1890)	136
WALTER PATER (1839–1894)	137
SIR WALTER RALEIGH (1552–1618)	140
JOHN RUSKIN (1819–1900)	143
SIR WALTER SCOTT (1771–1832)	146
ROBERT SOUTHEY (1774–1843)	148
HERBERT SPENCER (1820–1903)	150
ROBERT LOUIS STEVENSON (1850–1895)	153
WILLIAM MAKEPEACE THACKERAY (1811–1863)	161

CONTENTS

THE CLASSICS

ARISTOTLE (384 B.C. — 322 B.C.)	164
DEMETRIUS (345 B.C. — 283 B.C.)	168
DIONYSIUS (54 B.C. — 7 B.C.)	169
HORACE (65 B.C. — 8 B.C.)	171
PLATO (429 B.C. — 347 B.C.)	176

FRENCH WRITERS

HONORÉ DE BALZAC (1799–1850)	177
FRANÇOIS RENÉ VICOMTE DE CHATEAUBRIAND (1768–1848)	181
DENIS DIDEROT (1713–1784)	184
ALEXANDRE DUMAS (*Père*) (1802–1870)	188
GUSTAVE FLAUBERT (1821–1880)	192
ANATOLE FRANCE (1844–1924)	198
VICTOR HUGO (1802–1885)	200
JEAN DE LA FONTAINE (1621–1695)	205
PIERRE LOTI (1850–1923)	205
JEAN BAPTISTE POQUELIN MOLIÈRE (1622–1673)	206
MICHEL DE MONTAIGNE (1533–1592)	211
JEAN BAPTISTE RACINE (1639–1699)	213
JEAN JACQUES ROUSSEAU (1712–1778)	215
CHARLES AUGUSTIN SAINTE-BEUVE (1804–1869)	219
GEORGE SAND (1804–1876)	223
FRANÇOIS MARIE AROUET DE VOLTAIRE (1694–1778)	227

CONTENTS

GERMAN WRITERS

Johann Wolfgang von Goethe (1749–1832)	232
Heinrich Heine (1799–1856)	233
Gotthold Ephraim Lessing (1729–1781)	236
Friedrich Nietzsche (1844–1900)	238
Johann Christoph Friedrich von Schiller (1759–1805)	239
Arthur Schopenhauer (1788–1860)	243

ITALIAN WRITERS

Dante Alighieri (1265–1321)	248

SCANDINAVIAN WRITERS

Georg Brandes (1842–1927)	249
Henrik Ibsen (1828–1906)	252
August Strindberg (1849–1912)	255

RUSSIAN WRITERS

Fyodor Michailovitch Dostoevsky (1821–1881)	259
Nikolai Vasilievitch Gogol (1809–1852)	262
Alexander Pushkin (1799–1837)	265
Leo Tolstoi (1828–1910)	266
Ivan Turgeniev (1818–1883)	269

INTRODUCTION

In these brief but richly packed and crowded pages Mrs. Lincoln and Miss Smith have gathered together from all sorts of great writers the precepts and suggestions that seem of most use to those who would wish to make their own writing profitable and memorable. To be sure, there are times when, looking at the hundreds of thousands of young people who are aiming at literature, one feels that it would be kinder to discourage than to stimulate. I often get letters from young men and women who inquire passionately how they may become great poets, great novelists, even great biographers, if there are such things, and though I give them such suggestions as I can, I often think it might be wiser to advise them to become grocers or bond-salesmen or gunmen than to struggle for success in writing books. But I know well that when once the fever sets in, nothing will cure it or relieve it but experience, and these judicious editors have done their best to place the best experience of the world where these young people may easily get at it. In future, when I get such letters, I shall know where to turn.

As one looks over the comments of great writers on their own art, there are a few general lessons that strike one very strongly. First, there is the necessity of persistent, unremitting, undiscouraged, indefatigable labor.

The labor may be of very different kinds. Sometimes it is a matter of steady grind, with set hours, set methods, long aims pursued day in and day out to a far-flickering end. Sometimes it is in appearance much more casual, a matter of obeying moods and impulses and taking inspiration when it comes. But the laboring, toiling instinct is always there, even if its aspects vary. If you want to be a great author, you have got to work, and without work nothing great has ever been accomplished or ever will be.

Second, you have not only got to stick to your work, you have got to love it. There are perhaps occupations in which a man may succeed even if he has a distaste for them. Not so literature. The writer is an artist, if he is anything, and a mighty, haunting, pervading love for one's art is the condition of doing great things in it. Like other loves, this is sometimes perverse and restless and discontented. But it never dies, or if it does, the artist may make up his mind that he is dying too.

Another element of permanent literary success is sincerity. You may get temporary praise — and cash — by doing tricks, by playing a game, with deliberate intent to fool others and perhaps yourself. But you will take no pride in your work afterwards and others will have no enduring pleasure in it. You must write what you really think and feel. Your work must take a profound and lasting hold of you, if you are to convey any impression to others that is really worth while.

Again, and here is the greatest value of this collection,

INTRODUCTION

you must be catholic in your study of methods and masters. You must appreciate that very great work has been done by different men in very different ways. There is the improvising of Scott, of Dumas, of George Sand, of Trollope, the writer who pours out his inspiration with apparent divine ease, though perhaps underneath with more travail of spirit than he himself is always aware of. Again there is the toiling artist, like Flaubert, or Leopardi, or Stevenson, who spends hours, or days, or weeks, on what he is bound to have a few perfect pages. Do not be impatient or contemptuous of any of these methods, for all of them have often justified themselves by magnificent achievement. As with models for reading, so with these teachers, do not confine yourselves to any one and scorn the others. Hear what they all have to say, and take from each the suggestions that are best adapted to you.

But the lesson you will learn from all of them, the advice that all these great masters of the art will give you, each in his own way, is to be yourself. You may learn from any great writer who ever lived, and even from some very small ones. But do not make the greatest of masters an exclusive master or a model. You will learn from all of these wise and successful teachers and practitioners that the artist can have only one really enduring model, life. No matter whether it is Sophocles, or Dante, or Shakespeare, no matter whether it is Stevenson, or Henry James, or Bernard Shaw, they may all have sought the advice of their predecessors and heeded it and profited by it, but for all of them, and for a thousand others, the real teacher was their own hearts and the hearts of the men and women about them. Day after day, year after year, probe more and more deeply into the complex secrets of the human heart, study your own heart, study others' hearts, as illuminating and illuminated by your own, and let the product of that study pour itself out in such bewildering, simple richness as it will. But, though no teaching and no advice will take the place of the study of life, yet you will find you go at it with wider understanding and draw from it far greater profit when you have considered these suggestive pages which give the concentrated experience of those who have pursued the study with a zeal and a passion which you can never surpass.

GAMALIEL BRADFORD

THE WRITING ART
*Authorship as Experienced and
Expressed by the Great Writers*

THE WRITING ART

AMERICAN WRITERS

HENRY WARD BEECHER

I WANDERED out this morning under the trees (the good lady had gone to the village, and her daughter too; and I was quite free, and was shirking all work, and having a good time on the grass). That, you know, is a good way to write an article. It is bad to go out and look at things if you wish to write about them. You must let them look at you. You must show yourself to nature; walk about confidently and lovingly; gaze at just those things that have magnetism in them, or sympathy, or influence, or whatever you choose to call it. Then, after an hour or two, if you wish to write, go to your desk, and whatever has had a real hold upon you will then come vividly up like pictures,—just as it does to me now; and I should give you a sparkling, glorious article now, were it not that at this very nick of time I am interrupted by the word that, if I send in time for this week, I must send this minute. Oh, what you have lost! It was very fine — very — the thing I was about to do!

JOHN BURROUGHS

Men who write Journals are usually men of certain marked traits — they are idealists; they love solitude rather than society; they are self-conscious, and they love to write... their Journals largely take the place of social converse. Amiel, Emerson, and Thoreau, for example, were lonely souls, lacking in social gifts, and seeking relief in the society of their own thoughts. Such men go to their Journals as other men go to their clubs. They love to be alone with themselves, and dread to be benumbed or drained of their mental force by uncongenial persons. To such a man his Journal becomes his duplicate self, and he says to it what he could not say to his nearest friend. It becomes both an altar and a confessional.

It is a good thing to let your MS. matter stand a while before publishing; much sediment and personal conceit that was stirred up and held in solution during the freshet which it caused in your soul will settle from it and precipitate itself to the bottom.

Every good book has a spirit, a living, moving spirit, underlying and animating all its thought. Here is where its power is. This gives it an influence in the world greater than that of Cæsar or Alexander. This makes a book live. This brings Plato and Shakespeare down from age to age and makes them always new and inspiring. A poor book has not this spirit; it may have facts and truths, but, if they are not embedded in and animated by this spirit, it is but a mechanical contrivance and must soon sink to the bottom like all mud and sediment. But a live book, that is, one whose truths and principles float in spirit as a ship on the ocean, can never die. Some books have a great influence in the world that contain no very important facts. Such are spirit books, and they belong to what De Quincey terms the literature of power. Such are the writings of Milton, of Scott, of Shakespeare, and, in fact, all imaginative works. We read them, not to find facts of history, or science, or art, etc., but for the delicious spiritual power that flows into us from their pages. This beauty, or this real worth, cannot be shown by any craft of criticism; it eludes the most skillful analysis; it can be discerned only by tuning the soul to the same harmony. The same is true of a work of art, or a landscape.

Let me work all day in my garden, the next day ramble in the fields and woods, with a little reading, and the third day I can give myself to literary pursuits with a new freshness and vigor....

One of the secrets in writing, I find, is to choose a commanding position, a central stronghold, as it were, which easily commands long ranges and vast tracts of thought. An eminence, a high point. Then what progress one makes! he can't help but write well. At other times, when he gets entangled in the byways, as it were, how hard it is!

Many writers show great spirit and activity, dart out first this way, then that, but never arrive at any results. They show special merit, but never give any grand effects. Most of the criticism of the time is of this character; it is aimless; it leads nowhere. Writers cast about them vigorously, cutting right and left, but one easily sees that they are in a corner, or ravine, as it were, and do not command the ground about and beyond them.

... Thoreau preaches and teaches always. I never preach or teach. I simply see and describe. I must have a pure result. I paint the bird for its own sake, and for the pleasure it affords me, and am annoyed at any lesson or moral twist. Even the scholar in me (a very poor one he is!) must not show his head when I am writing on natural themes. I would remind of books no more than the things themselves do.

Finished my Signs and Seasons [the essay, not the book] today, begun two weeks ago. Writing is like fishing: you do not know that there are fish in the hole till you have caught them. I did not know there was an article in me on this subject till I fished it out. I tried many times before I had a bite, and I did much better some days than others. Stormy days (either snow or rain, though snow is best) were my best days. I did not know I had that bank article [1] in me till Gilder told me I had, and commanded me to write. The same is true of the Thoreau article, and, indeed, of nearly all my articles; they have been discoveries, and have surprised me.

As a writer, especially on literary themes, I suffer much from the want of a certain manly or masculine quality, the quality of self-assertion — strength and firmness of outline, of individuality. I am not easy and steady in my shoes. The common and vulgar form of the quality I speak of is called 'cheek.' But in the master writer it is firmness, dignity, composure — a steady unconscious assertion of his own personality. When I try to assert myself I waver and am painfully self-conscious, and fall into curious delusions; I think I have a certain strength and positiveness of character, but lack egoism. It is a family weakness; all my brothers are weak as men; do not make themselves felt for good or bad in the community. But this weakness of the *I* in me is probably a great help to me as a writer upon Nature. I do not stand in my own light. I am

[1] 'Broken Banks and Lax Directors,' *Century Magazine*, March, 1882.

pure spirit, pure feeling, and get very close to bird and beast. My thin skin lets the shy and delicate influences pass. I can surrender myself to Nature without effort. I am like her. That which hinders me with men, and makes me weak and ill at ease in their presence, makes me strong with impersonal Nature, and admits me to her influences. I lack the firm moral fibre of such men as Emerson and Carlyle. I am more tender and sympathetic than either, perhaps, but there is a plebeian streak in me, not in them. This again helps me with Nature, but hinders with men.

One important thing in writing is to divest yourself of any false or accidental mood, or view, or feeling, and get down to your real self, and speak as directly and sincerely as you do about your daily business and affairs, with as little affectation. One may write from the outside of his mind, as it were; write and write, learnedly and eloquently, and make no impression; but when he speaks from real insight and conviction of his own, men are always glad to hear him, whether they agree with him or not. Get down to your real self — your better real self — and let that speak. One's real self is always vital, and gives the impression of reality. So much writing and speaking is like machine-work. The Sunday sermon and the leading editorial are generally pieces of machine-work, as if you turned the crank and the discourse came out. It is not the man's real mind, his real experience. He does not know how to get at this; all is artificial, factitious; his garden is upon the housetop instead of upon the ground; his ideas have no root, no succulency, no flavor. He speaks from art, from culture, from faculty, and not from inspiration. How rare are real poems! poems that spring from real feeling, a real throb of emotion, and not from the mere itch of literary vanity!

Vital literature is not made by the study of literature, but by the study of things, of life.

EMILY DICKINSON

To Colonel T. W. Higginson

Dear Friend, — A letter always feels to me like Immortality because it is the mind alone without corporeal friend. Indebted in our talk to attitude and accent, there seems a spectral power in thought that walks alone. I would like to thank you for your great kindness, but never try to lift the words which I cannot hold.

If I read a book and it makes my whole body so cold no fire can ever warm me, I know that is poetry. If I feel physically as if the top of my head were taken off,

I know that is poetry. These are the only ways I know it. Is there any other way?

> A word left careless on a page
> May consecrate an eye,
> When folded in perpetual seam
> The wrinkled author lie.

To the same

Mr. Higginson, — Are you too deeply occupied to say if my verse is alive?

The mind is so near itself it cannot see distinctly, and I have none to ask.

Should you think it breathed, and had you the leisure to tell me, I should feel quick gratitude.

If I make the mistake, that you dared to tell me would give me sincerer honor toward you.

I enclose my name, asking you, if you please, sir, to tell me what is true?

That you will not betray me it is needless to ask, since honor is its own pawn.

To the same

Mr. Higginson, — Your kindness claimed earlier gratitude, but I was ill, and write today from my pillow.

Thank you for the surgery; it was not so painful as I supposed. I bring you others, as you ask, though they might not differ. While my thought is undressed, I can make the distinction; but when I put them in the gown, they look alike and numb.

You asked how old I was? I made no verse, but one or two, until this winter, sir.

I had a terror since September, I could tell to none; and so I sing, as the boy does of the burying ground, because I am afraid.

You inquire my books. For poets, I have Keats, and Mr. and Mrs. Browning. For prose, Mr. Ruskin, Sir Thomas Browne, and the 'Revelations.' I went to school, but in your manner of the phrase had no education. When a little girl, I had a friend who taught me Immortality; but venturing too near, himself, he never returned. Soon after my tutor died, and for several years my lexicon was my only companion. Then I found one more, but he was not contented I be his scholar, so he left the land.

You ask of my companions. Hills, sir, and the sundown, and a dog large as myself, that my father bought me. They are better than beings, because they know, but do not tell; and the noise in the pool at noon excels my piano.

I have a brother and sister; my mother does not care for thought, and father, too busy with his briefs to notice what we do. He buys me many books, but begs me not to read them, because he fears they joggle the mind. They are religious, except me, and address an eclipse, every morning, whom they call their 'Father.'

But I fear my story fatigues you. I would like to

learn. Could you tell me how to grow, or is it unconveyed, like melody or witchcraft?

You speak of Mr. Whitman. I never read his book, but was told that it was disgraceful.

I read Miss Prescott's Circumstance, but it followed me in the dark, so I avoided her.

Two editors of journals came to my father's house this winter, and asked me for my mind, and when I asked them 'why' they said I was penurious, and they would use it for the world.

I could not weight myself, myself. My size felt small to me. I read your chapters in the *Atlantic*, and experienced honor for you. I was sure you would not reject a confiding question.

Is this, sir, what you asked me to tell you?

To the same

Dear Friend, — Your letter gave no drunkenness, because I tasted rum before. Domingo comes but once; yet I have had few pleasures so deep as your opinion, and if I tried to thank you my tears would block my tongue.

My dying tutor told me that he would like to live till I had been a poet, but Death was much of mob as I could master, then. And when, far afterward, a sudden light on orchards, or a new fashion in the wind troubled my attention, I felt a palsy, here, the verses just relieve.

Your second letter surprised me, and for a moment, swung. I had not supposed it. Your first gave no dishonor, because the true are not ashamed. I thanked you for your justice, but could not drop the bells whose jingling cooled my tramp. Perhaps the balm seemed better, because you bled me first. I smile when you suggest that I delay 'to publish,' that being foreign to my thought as firmament to fin.

If fame belonged to me, I could not escape her; if she did not, the longest day would pass me on the chase, and the approbation of my dog would forsake me then. My barefoot rank is better.

You think my gait 'spasmodic.' I am in danger, sir. You think me 'uncontrolled.' I have no tribunal.

Would you have time to be the 'friend' you should think I need? I have a little shape: it would not crowd your desk, nor make much racket as the mouse that dents your galleries.

If I might bring you what I do — not so frequent to trouble you — and ask you if I told it clear, 'twould be control to me. The sailor cannot see the north, but knows the needle can. The 'hand you stretch me in the dark' I put mine in, and turn away. I have no Saxon now:

> As if I asked a common alms,
> And in my wondering hand
> A stranger pressed a kingdom,
> And I, bewildered, stand;
> As if I asked the Orient
> Had it for me a morn,

> And it should lift its purple dikes
> And shatter me with dawn!

But, will you be my preceptor, Mr. Higginson?

RALPH WALDO EMERSON

Poetry is the *gai science*. The trait and test of the poet is that he builds, adds, and affirms. The critic destroys: the poet says nothing but what helps somebody; let others be distracted with cares, he is exempt. All their pleasures are tinged with pain. All his pains are edged with pleasure. The gladness he imparts he shares. As one of the old Minnesingers sung, —

> Oft have I heard, and now believe it true,
> Whom man delights in, God delights in too.

Poetry is the consolation of mortal men. They live cabined, cribbed, confined, in a narrow and trivial lot, — in wants, pains, anxieties, and superstitions, in profligate politics, in personal animosities, in mean employments, — and victims of these; and the nobler powers untried, unknown. A poet comes, who lifts the veil; gives them glimpses of the laws of the universe; shows them the circumstance as illusion; shows that nature is only a language to express the laws, which are grand and beautiful, — and lets them, by his songs, into some of the realities. Socrates; the Indian teachers of the Maia; the Bibles of the nations; Shakspeare, Milton, Hafiz,

Ossian, the Welsh Bards, — these all deal with nature and history as means and symbols, and not as ends. With such guides they begin to see that what they had called pictures are realities, and the mean life is pictures. And this is achieved by words; for it is a few oracles spoken by perceiving men that are the texts on which religions and states are founded. And this perception has at once its moral sequence. Ben Jonson said, 'The principal end of poetry is to inform men in the just reason of living.'

Nothing so marks a man as imaginative expressions. A figurative statement arrests attention, and is remembered and repeated. How often has a phrase of this kind made a reputation. Pythagoras's Golden Sayings were such, and Socrates', and Mirabeau's, and Burke's, and Bonaparte's.

Great design belongs to a poem, and is better than any skill of execution, — but how rare! I find it in the poems of Wordsworth, — Laodamia, and the Ode to Dion, and the plan of The Recluse. We want design, and do not forgive the bards if they have only the art of enameling. We want an architect, and they bring us an upholsterer.

If your subject does not appear to you the flower of the world at this moment, you have not rightly chosen it.

You shall not read newspapers, nor politics, nor novels, nor Montaigne, nor the newest French book. You may read Plutarch, Plato, Plotinus, Hindoo mythology, and ethics. You may read Chaucer, Shakspeare, Ben Jonson, Milton, — and Milton's prose as his verse; read Collins and Gray; read Hafiz and the Trouveurs; nay, Welsh and British mythology of Arthur, and (in your ear) Ossian; fact-books, which all geniuses prize as raw material, and as antidote to verbiage and false poetry. Fact-books, if the facts be well and thoroughly told, are much more nearly allied to poetry than many books are that are written in rhyme.... Every book is good to read which sets the reader in a working mood. The deep book, no matter how remote the subject, helps us best.

The good writer seems to be writing about himself, but has his eye always on that thread of the universe which runs through himself, and all things.

I have found my advantage in going to a hotel with a task which could not prosper at home. I secured so a more absolute solitude.[1]... At home, the day is cut up into short strips. In the hotel, I forget rain, wind, cold, and heat. At home, I remember in my library the

---

[1] Much of this paragraph is omitted; it is printed in full in 'Inspiration' (*Letters and Social Aims*, pp. 288, 289).

wants of the farm, and have all too much sympathy. I envy the abstraction of some scholars I have known.... All the conditions must be right for my success, slight as that is. What untunes is as bad as what cripples or stuns me.

Therefore, I extol the prudence of Carlyle, who, for years, projected a library at the top of his house, high above the orbit of all housemaids, and out of earshot of doorbells. Could that be once secured, — a whole floor, — room for books, and a good bolt, — he could hope for six years of history, and he kept it in view till it was done....

BENJAMIN FRANKLIN

I would advise you to read with a pen in your hand, and enter in a little book short hints of what you find that is curious, or that may be useful; for this will be the best method of imprinting such particulars in your memory, where they will be ready, either for practice on some future occasion, if they are matters of utility; or at least to adorn and improve your conversation, if they are rather points of curiosity. And as many of the terms of science are such as you cannot have met with in your common reading, and may therefore be unacquainted with, I think it would be well for you to have a good dictionary at hand, to consult immediately when you meet with a word you do not comprehend the precise meaning of. This may at first seem troublesome and interrupting; but it is a trouble that will daily diminish, as you will daily find less and less occasion for your dictionary as you become more acquainted with the terms, and in the mean time you will read with more satisfaction, because with more understanding.

About this time [at age of fourteen] I met with an old volume of the Spectator. It was the third. I had never before seen any of them. I bought it. I thought the writing excellent, and wished, if possible, to imitate it. With this view I took some of the papers, and, making short hints of the sentiment in each sentence, laid them by a few days, and then, without looking at the book, tried to complete the papers again, by expressing each hinted sentiment at length, and as fully as it had been expressed before, in any suitable words that should come to hand. Then I compared my Spectator with the original, discovered some of my faults, and corrected them. But I found I wanted a stock of words, or a readiness in recollecting and using them, which I thought I should have acquired before that time if I had gone on making verses [as he had formerly done until his father discouraged him]; since the continual occasion for words of the same import, but of different length, to suit the measure, or of different sound for the rime, would have laid me under a constant necessity of searching for variety, and also have tended to fix that variety in my mind, and make me master of it. Therefore I took some of the tales and turned them into verses; and, after a time, when I had pretty well forgotten the prose, turned them back again. I also sometimes jumbled my collections of hints into confusion, and after some weeks endeavored to reduce them into the best order, before I began to form the full sentences and complete the paper. This was to teach me method in the arrangement of thoughts. By comparing my work afterwards with the original, I discovered many faults and amended them; but I sometimes had the pleasure of fancying that, in certain particulars of small import, I had been lucky enough to improve the method of the language, and this encouraged me to think that I might possibly in time come to be a tolerable English writer, of which I was extremely ambitious. My time for these exercises, and for reading was at night, after work or before it began in the morning, or on Sundays.

NATHANIEL HAWTHORNE

NOTES FOR NEW STORIES

A rich man left by will his mansion and estate to a poor couple. They remove into it, and find there a darksome servant, whom they are forbidden by will to turn away. He becomes a torment to them; and, in the finale, he turns out to be the former master of the estate.

Fortune to come like a pedlar with his goods — as wreaths of laurel, diamonds, crowns; selling them, but asking for them the sacrifice of health, of integrity, perhaps of life in the battlefield, and of the real pleasures of existence. Who would buy, if the price were to be paid down?

The dying exclamation of the Emperor Augustus, 'Has it not been well acted?' An essay on the misery of being always under a mask. Instances of people who wear masks in all classes of society, and never take them off even in the most familiar moments, though sometimes they may chance to slip aside.

A series of strange, mysterious, dreadful events to occur, wholly destructive of a person's happiness. He to impute them to various persons and causes, but ultimately finds that he is himself the sole agent. Moral, that our welfare depends on ourselves.

A person, while awake and in the business of life, to think highly of another, and place perfect confidence in him, but to be troubled with dreams in which this seeming friend appears to act the part of a most deadly enemy. Finally it is discovered that the dream-character is the true one. The explanation would be — the soul's instinctive perception.

Bees are sometimes drowned in the honey which they collect — so some writers lost in their collected learning.

My life only is a burden in the same way that it is to every toilsome man; and mine is a healthy weariness, such as needs only a night's sleep to remove it. But from henceforth forever I shall be entitled to call the sons of toil my brethren, and shall know how to sympathize with them, seeing that I likewise have risen at the dawn, and borne the fervor of the midday sun, nor turned my heavy footsteps homeward till eventide. Years hence, perhaps, the experience that my heart is acquiring now will flow out in truth and wisdom.

The only sensible ends of literature are, first, the pleasurable toil of writing; second, the gratification of one's family and friends; and, lastly, the solid cash.

It is odd enough that my own individual taste is for quite another class of novels than those which I myself am able to write. If I were to meet with such books as mine by another writer, I don't believe I should be able to get through them. Have you ever read the novels of Anthony Trollope? They precisely suit my taste; and through the inspiration of ale, are just as real as if some giant had hewn a great lump out of the earth, and put it under a glass case, with all its inhabitants going about their daily business, and not suspecting that they were made a show of.

O. HENRY
(SYDNEY PORTER)

A GUESS-PROOF MYSTERY STORY

The most popular and recent advertising dodge in literature is the Grand Guess Contest Mystery Story. Everybody is invited to guess how the story will end, at any time before the last chapter is published, and incidentally to buy a paper or subscribe. It is the easiest thing in the world to write a story of mystery that will defy the most ingenious guessers in the country.

To prove it, here is one that we offer $10,000 to any man and $15,000 to any woman who guesses the mystery before the last chapter.

The synopsis of the story is alone given, as literary style is not our object — we want mystery.

CHAPTER I

Judge Smith, a highly esteemed citizen of Plunkville, is found murdered in his bed at his home. He has been stabbed with a pair of scissors, poisoned with 'rough on rats.' His throat has been cut with an ivory handled razor, an artery in his arm has been opened, and he has been shot full of buckshot from a double-barreled gun.

The coroner is summoned and the room examined. On the ceiling is a bloody footprint, and on the floor are found a lady's lace handkerchief, embroidered with the initials 'J. B.,' a package of cigarettes and a ham sandwich. The coroner renders a verdict of suicide.

CHAPTER II

The judge leaves a daughter, Mabel, aged eighteen, and ravishingly lovely. The night before the murder she exhibited a revolver and an axe in the principal saloon in town and declared her intention of 'doing up' the old man. The judge has his life insured for $100,000 in her favor. Nobody suspects her of the crime.

Mabel is engaged to a young man named Charlie, who is seen on the night of the murder by several citizens climbing out the judge's window with a bloody razor and a shotgun in his hand. Society gives Charlie the cold shoulder.

A tramp is run over by a street car and before dying confesses to having committed the murder, and at the judge's funeral his brother, Colonel Smith, breaks down and acknowledges having killed the judge in order to get his watch. Mabel sends to Chicago and employs a skilled detective to work up the case.

CHAPTER III

A beautiful strange lady dressed in mourning comes to Plunkville and registers at the hotel as Jane Bumgartner. (The initials on the handkerchief!)

The next day a Chinaman is found who denies having killed the judge, and is arrested by the detective. The strange lady meets Charlie on the street, and, on smelling the smoke from his cigarette, faints. Mabel discards him and engages herself to the Chinaman.

CHAPTER IV

While the Chinaman is being tried for murder, Jane Bumgartner testifies that she saw the detective murder Judge Smith at the instance of the minister who conducted the funeral, and that Mabel is Charlie's stepmother. The Chinaman is about to confess when footsteps are heard approaching. The next chapter will be the last, and it is safe to say that no one will find it easy to guess the ending of the story. To show how difficult this feat is, the last chapter is now given.

CHAPTER V

The footsteps prove to be those of Thomas R. Hefflebomer of Washington Territory, who introduces positive proof of having murdered the judge during a fit of mental aberration, and Mabel marries a man named Tompkins, whom she met two years later at Hot Springs.

If I could have a thousand years — just one little thousand years — more of life, I might, in that time, draw near enough to true Romance to touch the hem of her robe.

Up from ships men come, and from waste places and forest and road and garret and cellar to maunder to me in strangely distributed words of the things they have seen and considered. The recording of their tales is no more than a matter of ears and fingers. There are only two fates I dread — deafness and writer's cramp.

This tribute to Bill Nye has the added interest of containing O. Henry's only known reference to humor as a whole:

Bill Nye, who recently laid down his pen for all time, was a unique figure in the field of humor. His best work probably more nearly represented American Humor than that of any other writer. Mr. Nye had a sense of the ludicrous that was keen and judicious. His humor was peculiarly American in that it depended upon sharp and unexpected contrasts and the bringing of opposites into unlooked for comparison for its effect. Again, he had the true essence of kindliness, without which humor is stripped of its greatest component part. His was the child's heart, the scholar's knowledge, and the philosopher's view of life. The world has been better for him, and when that can be said of a man the tears that drop upon his grave are more potent than the loud huzzas that follow the requiem of the greatest conqueror or the most successful statesman. The kindliest thoughts and the sincerest prayers follow the great humanitarian — for such he was — into the great beyond, and such solace as the hearty condolement of a million people can bring to the bereaved loved ones of Bill Nye is theirs.

OLIVER WENDELL HOLMES

Sometimes very young persons send communications which they want forwarded to editors; and these young persons do not always seem to have right conceptions of these same editors, and of the public, and of themselves. Here is a letter I wrote to one of these young folks, but, on the whole, thought it best not to send. It is not fair to single out one for such sharp advice, where there are hundreds that are in need of it.

Dear Sir, — You seem to be somewhat, but not a great deal, wiser than I was at your age. I don't wish to be understood as saying too much, for I think, without committing myself to any opinion on my present state, that I was not a Solomon at that stage of development.

You long to 'leap at a single bound into celebrity.' Nothing is so commonplace as to wish to be remarkable. Fame usually comes to those who are thinking about something else, — very rarely to those who say to themselves, 'Go to, now, let us be a celebrated individual!'

The struggle for fame, as such, commonly ends in notoriety; — that ladder is easy to climb, but it leads to the pillory which is crowded with fools who could not hold their tongues and rogues who could not hide their tricks.

If you have the consciousness of genius, do something to show it. The world is pretty quick, now-a-days, to catch the flavor of true originality; if you write anything remarkable, the magazines and newspapers will find you out, as the schoolboys find out where the ripe apples and pears are. Produce anything really good, and an intelligent editor will jump at it. Don't flatter yourself that any article of yours is rejected because you are unknown to fame. Nothing pleases an editor more than to get anything worth having from a new hand. There is always a dearth of really fine articles for a first-rate journal; for, of a hundred pieces received, ninety are at or below the sea-level; some have water enough, but no head; some head enough, but no water; only two or three are from full reservoirs, high up that hill which is so hard to climb.

You may have genius. The contrary is of course probable, but it is not demonstrated. If you have, the world wants you more than you want it. It has not only a desire, but a passion, for every spark of genius that shows itself among us; there is not a bullcalf in our national pasture that can bleat a rhyme but it is ten to one, among his friends, and no takers, that he is the real, genuine, no-mistake Osiris.

Qu'est-ce qu'il a fait? What has he done? That was

Napoleon's test. What have you done? Turn up the faces of your picture-cards, my boy! You need not make mouths at the public because it has not accepted you at your own fancy-valuation. Do the prettiest thing you can, and wait your time.

For the verses you sent me, I will not say they are hopeless, and I dare not affirm that they show promise. I am not an editor, but I know the standard of some editors. You must not expect to 'leap with a single bound' into the society of those whom it is not flattery to call your betters. When 'The Pactolian' has paid you for a copy of verses, — (I can furnish you a list of alliterative signatures, beginning with Annie Aureole and ending with Zoe Zenith), — when 'The Rag-bag' has stolen your piece, after carefully scratching your name out — when 'The Nutcracker' has thought you worth shelling, and strung the kernel of your cleverest poem — then, and not till then, you may consider the presumption against you, from the fact of your rhyming tendency, as called in question, and let our friends hear from you, if you think it worth while. You may possibly think me too candid, and even accuse me of incivility; but let me assure you that I am not half so plain-spoken as Nature, nor half so rude as Time. If you prefer the long jolting of public opinion to the gentle touch of friendship, try it like a man. Only remember this — that, if a bushel of potatoes is shaken in a market-cart without springs to it, the small potatoes always get to the bottom.

Believe me, etc., etc.

WILLIAM DEAN HOWELLS

From my own long experience as a magazine editor, I may say that the editor is more doubtful of failure in one who has once done well than of a second success. After all, the writer who can do but one good thing is rarer than people are apt to think in their love of the improbable; but the real danger with a young contributor is that he may become his own rival.

What would have been quite good enough from him in the first instance is not good enough in the second, because he has himself fixed his standard so high. His only hope is to surpass himself, and not begin resting on his laurels too soon; perhaps it is never well, soon or late, to rest upon one's laurels. It is well for one to make one's self scarce, and the best way to do this is to be more and more jealous of perfection in one's work.

The editor's conditions are that having found a good thing he must get as much of it as he can, and the chances are that he will be less exacting than the contributor imagines. It is for the contributor to be exacting, and to let nothing go to the editor as long as there is the possibility of making it better. He need not be afraid of being forgotten because he does not keep sending; the editor's memory is simply relentless; he could not forget the writer who has pleased him if he would, for such writers are few.

I do not believe that in my editorial service on the *Atlantic Monthly*, which lasted fifteen years in all, I forgot the name or the characteristic quality, or even the handwriting, of a contributor who had pleased me, and I forgot thousands who did not. I never lost faith in a contributor who had done a good thing; to the end I expected another good thing from him. I think I was always at least as patient with him as he was with me, though he may not have known it....

I know that, so far as I was concerned, the success of a young contributor was as precious as if I had myself written his paper or poem, and I doubt if it gave him more pleasure. The editor is, in fact, a sort of second self for the contributor, equally eager that he should stand well with the public, and able to promote his triumphs without egotism and share them without vanity.

I know from much suffering of my own that it is terrible to get back a manuscript, but it is not fatal, or I should have been dead a great many times before I was thirty, when the thing mostly ceased for me. One survives it again and again, and one ought to make the reflection that it is not the first business of a periodical to print contributions of this one or of that, but that its first business is to amuse and instruct its readers.

To do this it is necessary to print contributions, but whose they are, or how the writer will feel if they are not printed, cannot be considered. The editor can consider only what they are, and the young contributor will do well to consider that, although the editor may not be an infallible judge, or quite a good judge, it is his business to judge, and to judge without mercy. Mercy ought no more to qualify judgment in an artistic result than in a mathematical result.

I suppose, since I used to have it myself, that there is a superstition with most young contributors concerning their geographical position. I used to think that it was a disadvantage to send a thing from a small or unknown place, and that it doubled my insignificance to do so. I believed that if my envelope had borne the postmark of New York, or Boston, or some other city of literary distinction, it would have arrived on the editor's table with a great deal more authority. But I am sure this was a mistake from the first, and when I came to be an editor myself I constantly verified the fact from my own dealings with contributors.

A contribution from a remote and obscure place at once piqued my curiosity, and I soon learned that the fresh things, the original things, were apt to come from such places, and not from the literary centres.

One of the most interesting facts concerning the arts of all kinds is that those who wish to give their lives to them do not appear where the appliances for instruction in them exist. An artistic atmosphere does not create artists; a literary atmosphere does not create literators;

poets and painters spring up where there was never a verse made or a picture seen.

I think that every author who is honest with himself must own that his work would be twice as good if it were done twice. I was once so fortunately circumstanced that I was able entirely to rewrite one of my novels, and I have always thought it the best written, or at least indefinitely better than it would have been with a single writing. As a matter of fact, nearly all of them have been rewritten in a certain way. They have not actually been rewritten throughout, as in the case I speak of, but they have been gone over so often in manuscript and in proof that the effect has been much the same.

Unless you are sensible of some strong frame within your work, something vertebral, it is best to renounce it, and attempt something else in which you can feel it. If you are secure of the frame you must observe the quality and character of everything you build about it; you must touch, you must almost taste, you must certainly test, every material you employ; every bit of decoration must undergo the same scrutiny as the structure.

It will be some vague perception of the want of this vigilance in the young contributor's work which causes the editor to return it to him for revision, with those suggestions which he will do well to make the most of;

for when the editor once finds a contributor he can trust, he rejoices in him with a fondness which the contributor will never perhaps understand.

It will not do to write for the editor alone; the wise editor understands this, and averts his countenance from the contributor who writes at him; but if he feels that the contributor conceives the situation, and will conform to the conditions which his periodical has invented for itself, and will transgress none of its unwritten laws; if he perceives that he has put artistic conscience in every general and detail, and though he has not done the best, has done the best that he can do, he will begin to liberate him from every trammel except those he must wear himself, and will be only too glad to leave him free. He understands, if he is at all fit for his place, that a writer can do well only what he likes to do, and his wish is to leave him to himself as soon as possible.

People write because they wish to be known, or because they have heard that money is easily made in that way, or because they think they will chance that among a number of other things. The ignorance of technique which they often show is not nearly so disheartening as the palpable factitiousness of their product. It is something that they have made; it is not anything that has grown out of their lives.

I should think it would profit the young contributor,

before he puts pen to paper, to ask himself why he does so, and, if he finds that he has no motive in the love of the thing, to forbear.

Am I interested in what I am going to write about? Do I feel it strongly? Do I know it thoroughly? Do I imagine it clearly? The young contributor had better ask himself all these questions, and as many more like them as he can think of. Perhaps he will end by not being a young contributor.

If the young contributor finds that he has no delight in the thing he has attempted, he may very well give it up, for no one else will delight in it. But he need not give it up at once; perhaps his mood is bad; let him wait for a better, and try it again. He may not have learned how to do it well, and therefore he cannot love it, but perhaps he can learn to do it well.

The wonder and glory of art is that it is without formulas. Or, rather, each new piece of work requires the invention of new formulas, which will not serve again for another. You must apprentice yourself afresh at every fresh undertaking, and your mastery is always a victory over certain unexpected difficulties, and not a dominion of difficulties overcome before.

I believe, in other words, that mastery is merely the strength that comes of overcoming, and is never a sovereign power that smooths the path of all obstacles. The combinations in art are infinite, and almost never the same; you must make your key and fit it to each, and the key that unlocks one combination will not unlock another.

There is no royal road to excellence in literature, but the young contributor need not be dismayed at that. Royal roads are the ways that kings travel, and kings are mostly dull fellows, and rarely have a good time. They do not go along singing; the spring that trickles into the mossy log is not for them, nor

> The wildwood flower that simply blows.

But the traveler on the country road may stop for each of these; and it is not a bad condition of his progress that he must move so slowly that he can learn every detail of the landscape, both earth and sky, by heart.

The trouble with success is that it is apt to leave life behind, or apart. The successful writer especially is in danger of becoming isolated from the realities that nurtured in him the strength to win success. When he becomes famous, he becomes precious to criticism, to society, to all the things that do not exist from themselves, or have not the root of the matter in them.

Therefore, I think that a young writer's upward course should be slow and beset with many obstacles, even hardships. Not that I believe in hardships as having inherent virtues; I think it is stupid to regard them in that way; but they oftener bring out the virtues inherent in the sufferer from them than what I may call the *softships*; and at least they stop him, and give him time to think.

This is the great matter, for if we prosper forward rapidly, we have no time for anything but prospering forward rapidly. We have no time for art, even the art by which we prosper.

I would have the young contributor above all things realize that success is not his concern. Good work, true work, beautiful work is his affair, and nothing else. If he does this, success will take care of itself.

He has no business to think of the thing that will take. It is the editor's business to think of that, and it is the contributor's business to think of the thing that he can do with pleasure, the high pleasure that comes from the sense of worth in the thing done. Let him do the best he can, and trust the editor to decide whether it will take.

It will take far oftener than anything he attempts perfunctorily; and even if the editor thinks it will not take, and feels obliged to return it for that reason, he will return it with a real regret, with the honor and affection which we cannot help feeling for any one who has done a piece of good work, and with the will and the hope to get something from him that will take the next time, or the next, or the next.

WASHINGTON IRVING

THE AUTHOR'S ACCOUNT OF HIMSELF

I was always fond of visiting new scenes, and observing strange characters and manners. Even when a mere child I began my travels, and made many tours of discovery into foreign parts and unknown regions of my native city, to the frequent alarm of my parents, and the emolument of the town-crier. As I grew into boyhood, I extended the range of my observations. My holiday afternoons were spent in rambles about the surrounding country. I made myself familiar with all its places famous in history or fable. I knew every spot where a murder or robbery had been committed, or a ghost seen. I visited the neighboring villages, and added greatly to my stock of knowledge by noting their habits and customs, and conversing with their sages and great men. I even journeyed one long summer's day to the summit of the most distant hill, whence I stretched my eye over many a mile of *terra incognita*, and was astonished to find how vast a globe I inhabited.

This rambling propensity strengthened with my years. Books of voyages and travels became my passion, and in devouring their contents I neglected the regular exercises of the school. How wistfully would I wander about the pier-heads in fine weather, and watch the parting ships, bound to distant climes; with what longing eyes would I gaze after their lessening sails, and waft myself in imagination to the ends of the earth!

Further reading and thinking, though they brought this vague inclination into more reasonable bounds, only served to make it more decided. I visited various parts of my own country; and had I been merely a lover of fine scenery, I should have felt little desire to seek elsewhere its gratification, for on no country have the charms of nature been more prodigally lavished....

It has been either my good or evil lot to have my roving passion gratified. I have wandered through different countries, and witnessed many of the shifting scenes of life. I cannot say that I have studied them with the eye of a philosopher, but rather with the sauntering gaze with which humble lovers of the picturesque stroll from the window of one print-shop to another, caught sometimes by the delineations of beauty, sometimes by the distortions of caricature, and sometimes by loveliness of landscape. As it is the fashion for modern tourists to travel pencil in hand, and bring home their portfolios filled with sketches, I am disposed to get up a few for the entertainment of my friends. When, however, I look over the hints and memorandums I have taken down for the purpose, my heart almost fails me at finding how my idle humor has led me aside from the great objects studied by every regular traveler who would make a book. I fear I shall give equal disappointment with an unlucky landscape-painter, who had traveled on the Continent, but, following the bent of his vagrant inclination, had sketched in nooks, and corners, and by-places. His sketchbook was accordingly crowded with cottages, and landscapes, and obscure ruins; but he had neglected to paint St. Peter's; or the Coliseum; the cascade of Terni, or the bay of Naples; and had not a single glacier or volcano in his whole collection.

WILLIAM JAMES

To Henry James

Berlin, Sept. 26, 1867

Beloved 'Arry, — I hope you will not be severely disappointed on opening this fat envelope to find it is not all *letter*. I will first explain to you the nature of the enclosed document and then proceed to personal matters. The other day, as I was sitting alone with my deeply breached letter of credit, beweeping my outcast state, and wondering what I could possibly do for a living, it flashed across me that I might write a 'notice' of H. Grimm's novel which I had just been reading. To conceive with me is to execute, as you well know. And after sweating fearfully for three days, erasing, tearing my hair, copying, recopying, etc., etc., I have just succeeded in finishing the enclosed. I want you to read it, and if, after correcting the style and thoughts, with the aid of Mother, Alice, and Father, and rewriting it if possible, you judge it to be capable of interesting in any degree any one in the world but H. Grimm, himself, to send it to the Nation or the Round Table.

I feel that a living is hardly worth being gained at this price. Style is not my forte, and to strike the mean between pomposity and vulgar familiarity is indeed difficult. Still, an the rich guerdon accrue, an but ten beauteous dollars lie down on their green and glossy backs within the family treasury in consequence of my exertions, I shall feel glad that I have made them. I have not seen Grimm yet as he is in Switzerland. In his writings he is possessed of real imagination and eloquence, chiefly in an ethical line, and the novel is really distingué, somewhat as Cherbuliez's are, only with rather a deficiency on the physical and animal side. He is, to my taste, too idealistic, and Father would scout him for his arrant moralism. Goethe seems to have mainly suckled him, and the manner of this book is precisely that of Wilhelm Meister or Elective Affinities. There is something not exactly *robust* about him, but, *per contra*, great delicacy and an extreme belief in the existence and worth of truth and desire to attain it justly and impartially. In short, a rather painstaking liberality and want of careless animal spirits — which, by the bye, seem to be rather characteristics of the rising generation. But enough of him. The notice was mere taskwork. I could not get up a spark of interest in it, and I should not think it would be *d'actualité* for the Nation. Still, I could think of nothing else to do, and was bound to do something....

To Henry James

Chocorua, June 4, 1890

My dear Harry, —... The great event for me is the completion at last of my tedious book. I have been at my desk with it every day since I got back from Europe, and up at four in the morning with it for many a day of the last month. I have written every page four or five times over, and carried it 'on my mind' for nine years past, so you may imagine the relief. Besides, I am glad to appear at last as a man who has done something more than make phrases and projects. I will send you a copy, in the fall, I trust, though [the printer] is so inert about starting the proofs that we may not get through till midwinter or later. As 'Psychologies' go, it is a good one, but psychology is in such an antescientific condition that the whole present generation of them is predestined to become unreadable old medieval lumber, as soon as the first genuine tracks of insight are made. The sooner the better, for me!...

To W. D. Howells

Chocorua, Aug. 20, 1890

My dear Howells, — You've done it this time and no mistake! I've had a little leisure for reading this summer, and have just read, first your Shadow of a Dream, and next your Hazard of New Fortunes, and can hardly recollect a novel that has taken hold of me like the latter. Some compensations go with being a mature man, do they not? You couldn't possibly have done so solid a piece of work as that ten years ago, could you? The steady unflagging flow of it is something wonderful. Never a weak note, the number of characters, each intensely individual, the observation of detail, the everlasting wit and humor, and beneath all the bass accompaniment of the human problem, the entire Americanness of it, all make it a very great book, and one which will last when we shall have melted into the infinite azure. Ah! my dear Howells, it's worth something to be able to write such a book, and it is so peculiarly *yours* too, flavored with your idiosyncrasy.

To H. G. Wells

Cambridge, Nov. 28, 1908

Dear Wells, — First and Last Things is a great achievement. The first two 'books' should be entitled 'philosophy without humbug' and used as a textbook in all the colleges of the world. You have put your finger accurately on the true emphases, and — in the main — on what seem to me the true solutions (you are more monistic in your faith than I should be, but as long as you only call it 'faith,' that's your right and privilege), and the simplicity of your statements ought to make us 'professionals' blush. I have been 35 years on the way to similar conclusions — simply because I started as a professional and had to *débrouiller* them from all the traditional school rubbish.

The other two books exhibit you in the character of the Tolstoy of the English world. A sunny and healthy-minded Tolstoy, as he is a pessimistic and morbid-minded Wells. Where the 'higher synthesis' will be born, who shall combine the pair of you, Heaven only knows. But you are carrying on the same function, not only in that neither of your minds is boxed and boarded up like the mind of an ordinary human being, but all the contents down to the very bottom come out freely and unreservedly and simply, but in that you both have the power of contagious speech, and set the similar mood vibrating in the reader. Be happy in that such power has been put into your hands! This book is worth any 100 volumes on Metaphysics and any 200 of Ethics, of the ordinary sort.

HENRY WADSWORTH LONGFELLOW

How different from this gossip is the divine Dante, with which I begin the morning! I write a few lines every day before breakfast. It is the first thing I do, — the morning prayer, the key-note of the day.... I really have but a few moments to devote to it daily; yet daily a stone, small or great, is laid upon the pile.

As to intellectual matter, I have not done much since I left you. A half-dozen poems on Slavery, written at sea, and a translation of sixteen cantos of Dante, is all I have accomplished in that way. I agree with you entirely in what you say about translations. It is like running a ploughshare through the soil of one's mind; a thousand germs of thought start up (excuse this agricultural figure), which otherwise might have lain and rotted in the ground. Still, it sometimes seems to me like an excuse for being lazy, — like leaning on another man's shoulder.

I am just beginning the publication of a volume of specimens of foreign poetry, — being a selection of the best English translations from the Anglo-Saxon, Icelandic, Danish, Swedish, German, Dutch, French, Italian, Spanish, and Portuguese. The object of the book is to bring together in one volume what is now scattered through a hundred, and not easily got at.

I shall write the introductions. Most of the translations, of course, will be by other hands.

11th. Wrote a sonnet on Autumn.

12th. Began a poem on a clock, with the words, 'Forever, never' as the burden; suggested by the words of Bridaine, the old French missionary, who said of eternity, '*C'est une pendule dont le balancier dit et redit sans cesse ces deux mots seulement dans le silence des tombeaux, — Toujours, jamais! Jamais, toujours! Et pendant ces effroyables révolutions, un réprouvé s'écrie, "Quelle heure est-il?" et la voix d'un autre miserable lui répond, "L'Éternité."* '

13th. Walked in the garden and tried to finish the Ode to a Child; but could not find the exact expressions I wanted, to round and complete the whole.

14th. Felt more than ever today the difference between my ideal home-world of Poetry, and the outer, actual, tangible Prose world. When I go out of the precincts of my study, down the village street to college, how the scaffoldings about the Palace of Song come rattling and clattering down!

16th. Before church, wrote The Arrow and the Song, which came into my mind as I stood with my back to the fire, and glanced on to the paper with arrowy speed. Literally an improvisation.

19th. After all, old Chateaubriand is a glowing writer. His description of the French, in the *Études Historiques*, is graphic and true. Niagara is also well sketched, —...

27th. In the evening the Club supped here; the first time we have been together for many months. A pity these meetings should be so interrupted, as much good comes of our discussions and friendly comparison of opinions.

11th. In a newspaper a high-strung article on Festus; with introduction stating that 'the Age is still waiting for its Poet' — one who should be hailed by acclamation as the Seer of this nineteenth century. Was ever a poet acknowledged by his age as its poet? Do the critics expect his advent heralded by signs and wonders? Or will he, too, come 'like a thief in the night'? In the evening began reading The Wandering Jew. Large canvas, and bold strokes with a coarse brush.

9th. Tried a pipe, after long abstinence. Not very pleasant. Decidedly, the calm, dull husbanding of one's nervous energies though less conducive to swift intellectual effort, is more so to happiness. Let us be calm and happy, rather than excitable and *nervous-minded*. In the evening, Fichte's Lectures on the Nature of the Scholar, — very interesting, with its doctrine of the 'Divine Idea,' which is like Swedenborg. It dwells more or less with every one, and to it must every scholar conform himself.

25th. Authors and artists of every kind have one element of unhappiness in their lot, namely, the disproportion between their designs and their deeds. Even the greatest cannot execute one tenth part of what they conceive.

11th. I am in despair at the swift flight of time, and the utter impossibility I feel to lay hold upon anything permanent. All my hours and days go to perishable things. College takes half the time; and other people, with their interminable letters and poems and requests and demands, take the rest. I have hardly a moment to think of my own writings, and am cheated of some of life's fairest hours. This is the extreme of folly; and if I knew a man, far off in some foreign land, doing as I do here, I should say he was mad.

JAMES RUSSELL LOWELL

Those who look upon language only as anatomists of its structure, or who regard it as only a means of conveying abstract truth from mind to mind, as if it were so many algebraic formulae, are apt to overlook the fact that its being alive is all that gives it poetic value. We do not mean what is technically called a living language, — the contrivance, hollow as a speaking-trumpet, by which breathing and moving bipeds, even now, sailing o'er life's solemn main, are enabled to hail each other and make known their mutual shortness of mental stores,—but one that is still hot from the hearts and brains of a people, not hardened yet, but moltenly ductile to new shapes of sharp and clear relief in the moulds of new thought. So soon as a language has become literary, so soon as there is a gap between the speech of books and that of life, the language becomes, so far as poetry is concerned, almost as dead as Latin, and (as in writing Latin verses) a mind in itself essentially original becomes in the use of such a medium of utterance unconsciously reminiscential and reflective, lunar and not solar, in expression and even in thought. For words and thoughts have a much more intimate and genetic relation, one with the other, than most men have any notion of; and it is one thing to use our mother-tongue as if it belonged to us, and another to be the puppets of an overmastering vocabulary.

The final judgment of the world is intuitive, and is based, not on proof that a work possesses some of the qualities of another whose greatness is acknowledged, but on the immediate feeling that it carries to a high point of perfection certain qualities proper to itself. One does not flatter a fine pear by comparing it to a fine peach, nor learn what a fine peach is by tasting ever so many poor ones. The boy who makes his first bite into one does not need to ask his father if or how or why it is good. Because continuity is a merit in some kinds of writing, shall we refuse ourselves to the authentic charm of Montaigne's want of it? I have heard people complain of French tragedies because they were so very French. This, though it may not be to some particular tastes, and may from one point of view be a defect, is from another and far higher a distinguished merit. It is their flavor, as direct a telltale of the soil whence they drew it as that of French wines is. Suppose we should tax the Elgin marbles with being too Greek? When will people, nay, when will even critics, get over this self-defrauding trick of cheapening the excellence of one thing by that of another, this conclusive style of judgment which consists simply in belonging to the other parish? As one grows older, one loses many idols, perhaps comes at last to have none at all, though he may honestly enough uncover in deference to the worshippers before any shrine. But for the seeming loss the compensation is ample. These saints of literature descend from their canopied remoteness to be even more precious as men like ourselves, our companions in field and street, speaking the same tongue, though in many dialects, and owning one creed under the most diverse masks of form.

The first demand we make upon whatever claims to be a work of art (and we have a right to make it) is that it shall be *in keeping*. Now this propriety is of two kinds, either extrinsic or intrinsic. In the first I should class whatever relates rather to the body than the soul of the work, such as fidelity to the facts of history (wherever that is important), congruity of costume, and the like, — in short, whatever might come under the head of *picturesque* truth, a departure from which would shock too rudely our preconceived associations. I have seen an Indian chief in French boots, and he seemed to me almost tragic; but, put upon the stage in tragedy, he would have been ludicrous. Lichtenberg, writing from London in 1775, tells us that Garrick played Hamlet in a suit of the French fashion, then commonly worn, and that he was blamed for it by some of the critics; but, he says, one hears no such criticism during the play, nor on the way home, nor at supper afterwards, nor indeed till the emotion roused by the great actor has had time to subside. He justifies Garrick, though we should not be able to endure it now. Yet nothing would be gained by trying to make Hamlet's costume true to the assumed period of the play, for the scene of it is laid in a Denmark that has no dates.

In the second and more important category, I should put, first, co-ordination of character, that is, a certain variety in harmony of the personages of a drama, as in the attitudes and coloring of the figures in a pictorial composition, so that, while mutually relieving and setting off each other, they shall combine in the total impression; second, that subordinate truth to Nature which makes each character coherent in itself; and, third, such propriety of costume and the like as shall satisfy the superhistoric sense, to which, and to which alone, the higher drama appeals. All these come within the scope of *imaginative* truth.

WORDSWORTH, KEATS, BYRON

Three men, almost contemporaneous with each other — Wordsworth, Keats, and Byron — were the great means of bringing back English poetry from the sandy deserts of rhetoric, and recovering for her her triple inheritance of simplicity, sensuousness, and passion. Of these, Wordsworth was the only conscious reformer, and his hostility to the existing formalism injured his earlier poems by tinging them with something of iconoclastic extravagance. He was the deepest thinker, Keats the most essentially a poet, and Byron the most keenly intellectual of the three. Keats had the broadest mind, or at least his mind was open on more sides, and he was able to understand Wordsworth and judge Byron, equally conscious, through his artistic sense, of the greatnesses of the one and the many littlenesses of the other, while Wordsworth was isolated in a feeling of his prophetic character, and Byron had only an uneasy and jealous instinct of contemporary merit. The poems of Wordsworth, as he was the most individual, accordingly reflect the moods of his own nature; those of Keats, from sensitiveness of organization, the moods of his own taste and feeling; and those of Byron, who was impressible chiefly through the understanding, the intellectual and moral wants of the time in which he lived. Wordsworth has influenced most the ideas of succeeding poets; Keats, their forms; and Byron, interesting to men of imagination less for his writings than for what his writings indicate, reappears no more in poetry, but presents an ideal to youth made restless with vague desires not yet regulated by experience nor supplied with motives by the duties of life.

EDGAR ALLAN POE

I have often thought how interesting a magazine paper might be written by any author who would — that is to say, who could — detail, step by step, the processes by which any one of his compositions attained its ultimate point of completion. Why such a paper has never been given to the world, I am much at a loss to say; but, perhaps, the autorial vanity has had more to do with the omission than any one other cause. Most writers — poets in especial — prefer having it understood that they compose by a species of fine frenzy — an ecstatic intuition — and would positively shudder at letting the public take a peep behind the scenes, at the elaborate and vacillating crudities of thought — at the true purposes seized only at the last moment — at the innumerable glimpses of idea that arrived not at the maturity of full view — at the fully matured fancies discarded in despair as unmanageable — at the cautious selections and rejections — at the painful erasures and interpolations — in a word, at the wheels and pinions —

the tackle for scene-shifting — the stepladders and demon-traps — the cock's feathers, the red paint and the black patches, which, in ninety-nine cases out of the hundred, constitute the properties of the literary *histrio*.

I am aware, on the other hand, that the case is by no means common in which an author is at all in condition to retrace the steps by which his conclusions have been attained. In general, suggestions, having arisen pell-mell, are pursued and forgotten in a similar manner.

For my own part, I have neither sympathy with the repugnance alluded to, nor at any time the least difficulty in recalling to mind the progressive steps of any of my compositions; and since the interest of any analysis, or reconstruction, such as I have considered a desideratum, is quite independent of any real or fancied interest in the thing analyzed, it will not be regarded as a breach of decorum on my part to show the *modus operandi* by which some of my own works were put together. I select The Raven, as most generally known. It is my design to render it manifest that no one point in its composition is referable either to accident or intuition, — that the work proceeded, step by step, to its completion with the precision and rigid consequence of a mathematical problem.

Let us dismiss, as irrelevant to the poem, per se, the circumstance — or say the necessity — which, in the first place, gave rise to the intention of composing a poem that should suit at once the popular and critical taste.

We commence, then, with this intention.

The initial consideration was that of extent. If any literary work is too long to be read at one sitting, we must be content to dispense with the immensely important effect derivable from unity of impression; for, if two sittings be required, the affairs of the world interfere, and everything like totality is at once destroyed. But since, *ceteris paribus*, no poet can afford to dispense with anything that may advance his design, it but remains to be seen whether there is, in extent, any advantage to counterbalance the loss of unity which attends it. Here I say no, at once. What we term a long poem is, in fact, merely a succession of brief ones, — that is to say, of brief poetical effects. It is needless to demonstrate that a poem is such, only inasmuch as it intensely excites, by elevating, the soul; and all intense excitements are, through a psychal necessity, brief. For this reason, at least one half of the Paradise Lost is essentially prose, — a succession of poetical excitements interspersed, inevitably, with corresponding depressions, — the whole being deprived, through the extremeness of its length, of the vastly important artistic element, totality, or unity, of effect.

It appears evident, then, that there is a distinct limit, as regards length, to all works of literary art, — the limit of a single sitting, — and that, although in certain classes of prose composition such as Robinson Crusoe, (demanding no unity) this limit may be advantageously overpassed, it can never properly be overpassed in a poem. Within this limit, the extent of a poem may be made to bear mathematical relation to its merit, — in other words, to the excitement or elevation, — again, in other words, to the degree of the true poetical effect which it is capable of inducing; for it is clear that the brevity must be in direct ratio of the intensity of the intended effect: this, with one proviso — that a certain degree of duration is absolutely requisite for the production of any effect at all.

Holding in view these considerations, as well as that degree of excitement which I deemed not above the popular, while not below the critical, taste, I reached at once what I conceived the proper length for my intended poem, — a length of about one hundred lines. It is, in fact, a hundred and eight.

My next thought concerned the choice of an impression, or effect, to be conveyed: and here I may as well observe that, throughout the construction, I kept steadily in view the design of rendering the work universally appreciable. I should be carried too far out of my immediate topic were I to demonstrate a point upon which I have repeatedly insisted, and which, with the poetical, stands not in the slightest need of demonstration, — the point, I mean, that Beauty is the sole legitimate province of the poem. A few words, however, in elucidation of my real meaning, which some of my friends have evinced a disposition to misrepresent. That pleasure which is at once the most intense, the most elevating, and the most pure, is, I believe, found in the contemplation of the beautiful. When, indeed, men speak of Beauty, they mean, precisely, not a quality, as is supposed, but an effect, — they refer, in short, just to that intense and pure elevation of soul — not of intellect, or of heart — upon which I have commented, and which is experienced in consequence of contemplating 'the beautiful.' Now I designate Beauty as the province of the poem, merely because it is an obvious rule of Art that effects should be made to spring from direct causes, — that objects should be attained through means best adapted for their attainment, — no one as yet having been weak enough to deny that the peculiar elevation alluded to is most readily attained in the poem. Now the object Truth, or the satisfaction of the intellect, and the object Passion, or the excitement of the heart, are, although attainable to a certain extent, in poetry, far more readily attainable in prose. Truth, in fact, demands a precision, and Passion a homeliness (the truly passionate will comprehend me) which are absolutely antagonistic to that Beauty which, I maintain, is the excitement, or pleasurable elevation, of the soul. It by no means follows from anything here said, that passion, or even truth, may not be introduced, and even profitably introduced, into a poem — for they may serve in elucidation, or aid the general effect, as do discords in music, by contrast, — but the true artist will always contrive, first, to tone them into proper subservience to the predominant aim, and, secondly, to enveil them, as far as possible, in that Beauty which is the atmosphere and the essence of the poem.

Regarding, then, Beauty as my province, my next question referred to the tone of its highest manifestation, — and all experience has shown that this tone is one of sadness. Beauty of whatever kind, in its supreme development, invariably excites the sensitive soul to tears. Melancholy is thus the most legitimate of all the poetical tones.

JAMES WHITCOMB RILEY

To Mrs. R. E. Jones

Aug. 4, 1880

Dear Friend: I'm 'most afraid you're spoiling me with all your good words, praises and encores, and tincturing me, too, beyond my wont with that delirious favoring — enthusiasm — that leaps and revels so along your veins that my own twang and tingle as I write. And I'm going to follow your advice — for this morning at least — and not attempt a line of verse until I shall have answered your best of letters and the soul it held. 'You are glad you are an enthusiast,' and I'm glad, too, — 'cause even though your lavish praise may stimulate an egotism as alert as mine, still that is just the spirit that needs active exercise, and should by no means lie dormant, as you seem to think in your case, — 'To write my best, only for the sake of beholding it in print seemed egotistical to me.' — 'And there are so many writers in the field there doesn't appear to be room for all.' — Make room, then, and for yourself — and I do assure you that you can't do that, no matter what your worth, without the strongest consciousness of that worth yourself, and the continued emphasis of that fact in your bearing toward the public, and in all you undertake, — and that may doubtless be called 'egotism,' — let 'em call it what they will — the more you possess of it, the sooner you will shake hands with Success is my serious belief. But, ah! you say — 'A man can wave his hat and shout bravo! and a woman she can' — just strike hands with him and climb right on to glory by his side — if she has only strength — as Mrs. Browning — the God-woman — to conquer her own modesty and self-disparagement, and let the great strong, towering soul step out and straighten-up among the stars. And what a glorious giant she is then! — I gather from your letters and your poems that it is your desire to reach, at last, *some height*, at least, along the upward path. And this is why I have spoken, and will speak, most seriously.

More than four years ago I received a letter from J. T. Trowbridge responding to my query as to how I might find market for my verse. I was then, as now you are, writing gratuitously, but hungrier a thousand times, I know, for some crumb of pecuniary help, and recompense for my work. — And Trowbridge said in order to make poetry marketable in this day and age it must be a part of it — that is, it must possess the qualities of the great Present: dash, brilliancy, strength, originality — and always a marked individuality of its own — a striking something that would stamp it from the ordinary. These are not his words — but the meaning of them as nearly as I can give it after the constant endeavor of years to follow his advice. Then it was not long till some hint of real success came dawning — not in the East, however, where naturally one looks for dawn — but here in the West, where are so many papers seemingly eager to advance and lend assistance to the poor bedrabbled strugglers in the ever-standing army of poets, jingle-ringers, and verse-carpenters. Since then, I have been steadily gaining, until now — with the exception of one magazine and paper of the East — I have more engagements for verse alone here in my western home than I can fill creditably — the pay not much, but still enough to humor some extravagances, and steadily increasing. Another thing I speak of before leaving this *modus-operandi* outline of how I write for market — and that is: We are writing for today and for the general reader — who, by the bye, is anything but a profound or classical scholar. Therefore, it has been, and is, my effort to avoid all phrases, words or reference of the old-time order of literature; and to avoid, too, the very acquaintance of it — because we are apt to absorb more or less of the peculiar ideas, methods, etc., of those authors we read; and as everything is right in its place — so the old authors are right in the past — while new ones must be here in the present — see? Whenever I am forced to say a commonplace thing it is my effort, at least, to say it as it never has been said before — if such a thing can be done without an apparent strain. Then, too, as before intimated, I exercise just all the egotism at command (not a small stock, I assure you), and try to believe myself as smart, or smarter, than anybody else who ever attempted doing anything; and, as a usual thing, to counteract the many dangers likely to result from such indulgence, I lay my work aside, as first perfected, forget it as wholly as I can, and the next day, perhaps, resurrect it in a mood the very opposite of that in which it was produced, and coldly, cruelly and most relentlessly attack and tear it into all possible shreds, — then when Mr. Public gets it, if the critic can find meaner treatment to bestow on it than I have given, he must have a very wicked heart indeed, and I a very tender one, if what he says of it can sting the least.

To Benj. S. Parker

Greenfield, Ind.
August 29, 1887

Dear Parker: Just as your letter came I was called from town, and so till now I have been kept from answering it.

In many respects I agree with you regarding dialect — Yankee, Southern, Hoosier and all the rest; still I most conscientiously believe (outside of all its numberless deviations) there is a legitimate use for it, and as honorable a place for it as for the English, pure and unadulterated. The only trouble seems to be its misuse

— its use by writers who fail wholly to interpret its real spirit and character either through blind ignorance, or malicious perverseness, in what they are about. To range back to the very Genesis of all speech, we can only righteously conjecture a dialectic tongue — a deduction as natural as that a babe must first lisp — the child babble — and the youth and man gradually educate away all like preceding blemishes, and I think it is absolutely necessary, in the general illustration of human life and character, to employ the dialect as the speech refined — its real value, of course, dependent on the downright wisdom and honesty of the writer who employs it. And my ambition in the use of dialect is simply as above outlined. That I have few endorsers among the scholarly I grievedly admit, yet am graciously assured and compensated by the homely approbation of my class and grade of fellowmen. Once in a while, however (and there's, at last, a discernible growth of the tendency), some finished critic discriminates and estimates the dialectic purpose exactly. Let me quote from *Art Interchange* of August thirteenth:

It says of a dialect poem of mine in August *Century* that it 'is an illustration of the only possible excuse for this sort of work,' in that 'the tender and touching little poem does not depend on the dialect' — but that — 'The feeling, the homely pathos of the verse makes it of value, and the dialect is simply its strongest and most fitting expression.' Now I am very proud of this detailed estimate of the poem. That is the highest praise

I seek or my ambition desires, and I think you will believe me and approve me there.

HENRY D. THOREAU

Nov. 20, 1857. In books, that which is most generally interesting is what comes home to the most cherished private experience of the greatest number. It is not the book of him who has traveled farthest on the surface of the globe, but of him who has lived the deepest, and been the most at home. If an equal emotion is excited by a familiar homely phenomenon as by the pyramids, there is no advantage in seeing the pyramids. It is on the whole better, as it is simpler, to use the common language. We require that the reporter be very firmly planted before the facts which he observes, not a mere passer-by, hence the facts cannot be too homely. A man is worth most to himself and to others, whether as an observer, or poet, or neighbor, or friend, who is most contented and at home. There his life is the most intense, and he loses the fewest moments. Familiar and surrounding objects are the best symbols and illustrations of his life. If a man who has had deep experiences should endeavor to describe them in a book of travels, it would be to use the language of a wandering tribe instead of a universal language. The poet has made the best roots in his native soil, and is the hardest to transplant. The man who is often thinking that it would be better to be somewhere else than where he is, excommunicates himself. Here I have been these forty years learning the language of these fields that I may the better express myself. If I should travel to the prairies I should much less understand them, and my past life would serve me but ill to describe them. Many a weed stands for more of life to me than the big trees of California would if I should go there. We need only travel enough to give our intellects an airing. In spite of Malthus and the rest, there will be plenty of room in this world, if every man will mind his own business. I have not heard of any planet running against another yet.

It is surprising how much, from the habit of regarding writing as an accomplishment, is wasted on form. A very little information or wit is mixed up with a great deal of conventionalism in the style of expressing it, as with a sort of preponderating paste or vehicle. Some life is not simply expressed, but a long-winded speech is made, with an occasional attempt to put a little life into it.

Improve every opportunity to express yourself in writing, as if it were your last.

Say the thing with which you labor. It is a waste of time for the writer to use his talents merely. Be faithful to your genius. Write in the strain that interests you most. Consult not the popular taste.

Nov. 12, 1851. Write often, write upon a thousand themes, rather than long at a time, not trying to turn too many feeble summersets in the air, and so come down upon your head at last. Antæus-like, be not long absent from the ground. Those sentences are good and well-discharged which are like so many little resiliences from the spring-floor of our life, each a distinct fruit and kernel springing from *terra firma*. Let there be as many distinct plants as the soil and the light can maintain. Take as many bounds in a day as possible, sentences uttered with your back to the wall. Those are the admirable bounds when the performer has lately touched the spring-board. A good bound into the air from the air is a good and wholesome experience, but what shall we say to a man's leaping off precipices in the attempt to fly? He comes down like lead. But let your feet be planted upon the rock, with the rock also at your back, and as in the case of King James and Roderick Dhu, you can say, —

> Come one, come all, this rock shall fly
> From its firm base, as soon as I.

Such, uttered or not, is the strength of your sentences in which there is no strain, no fluttering inconstant and quasi aspiration, and ever memorable Icarian fall wherein your helpless wings are expanded merely by your swift descent into the pelagos beneath.

In writing, conversation should be folded many times thick. It is the height of art that, on the first perusal, plain common sense should appear; on the second, severe truth; and on the third, beauty; and, having these warrants for its depth and reality, we may then enjoy the beauty for evermore.

His style,[1] as I remember, is singularly vague (I refer to the book), and, before I got to the end of the sentences, I was off the track. If you indulge in long periods, you must be sure to have a snapper at the end. As for style of writing, if one has anything to say, it drops from him simply and directly, as a stone falls to the ground. There are no two ways about it, but down it comes, and he may stick in the points and stops wherever he can get a chance. New ideas come into this world somewhat like falling meteors, with a flash and an explosion, and perhaps somebody's castle-roof perforated.

MARK TWAIN

(SAMUEL LANGHORNE CLEMENS)

... Shortly after my marriage, in 1870, I received a letter from a young man in St. Louis who was possibly a

[1] Wilson Flagg, a writer on scenery and natural history.

distant relative of mine — I don't remember now about that — but his letter said that he was anxious and ambitious to become a journalist — and would I send him a letter of introduction to some St. Louis newspaper and make an effort to get him a place as a reporter? It was the first time I had had an opportunity to make a new trial of my great scheme. I wrote him and said I would get him a place on any newspaper in St. Louis; he could choose the one he preferred, but he must promise me to faithfully follow out the instructions which I should give him. He replied that he would follow out those instructions to the letter and with enthusiasm. His letter was overflowing with gratitude — premature gratitude. He asked for the instructions. I sent them. I said he must not use a letter of introduction from me or from any one else. He must go to the newspaper of his choice and say that he was idle, and weary of being idle, and wanted work — that he was pining for work, longing for work — that he didn't care for wages, didn't want wages, but would support himself; he wanted work, nothing but work, and not work of a particular kind, but any kind of work they would give him to do. He would sweep out the editorial rooms; he would keep the inkstands full, and the mucilage bottles; he would run errands; he would make himself useful in every way he could.

I suspected that my scheme would not work with everybody — that some people would scorn to labor for nothing and would think it matter for self-contempt;

also that many persons would think me a fool to suggest such a project; also that many persons would not have character enough to go into the scheme in a determined way and test it. I was interested to know what kind of a candidate this one was, but of course I had to wait some time to find out. I had told him he must never ask for wages; he must never be beguiled into making that mistake; that sooner or later an offer of wages would come from somewhere, and in that case he must go straight to his employer and give him the opportunity to offer him the like wages, in which case he must stay where he was — that as long as he was in anybody's employ he must never ask for an advance of wages; that would always come from somewhere else if he proved his worthiness.

The scheme worked again. That young fellow chose his paper, and during the first few days he did the sweeping out and other humble work, and kept his mouth shut. After that the staff began to take notice of him. They saw that they could employ him in lots of ways that saved time and effort for them at no expense. They found that he was alert and willing. They began presently to widen his usefulness. Then he ventured to risk another detail of my instructions; I had told him not to be in a hurry about it, but to make his popularity secure first. He took up that detail now. When he was on his road between office and home, and when he was out on errands, he kept his eyes open, and whenever he saw anything that could be useful in the local columns he wrote it out, then went over it and abolished adjectives, went over it again and extinguished other surplusages, and finally when he got it boiled down to the plain facts with the ruffles and other embroideries all gone, he laid it on the city editor's desk. He scored several successes, and saw his stuff go into the paper unpruned. Presently the city editor when short of help sent him out on an assignment; he did his best with it, and with good results. This happened with more and more frequency. It brought him into contact with all the reporters of all the newspapers. He made friends with them and presently one of them told him of a berth that was vacant, and that he could get it and the wages too. He said he must see his own employers first about it. In strict accordance with my instructions he carried the offer to his own employers, and the thing happened which was to be expected. They said they could pay that wage as well as any other newspaper — stay where he was.

This young man wrote me two or three times a year and he always had something freshly encouraging to report about my scheme. Now and then he would be offered a raise by another newspaper. He carried the news to his own paper; his own paper stood the raise every time and he remained there. Finally he got an offer which his employers could not meet, and then they parted. This offer was a salary of three thousand a year, to be managing editor on a daily in a Southern city of considerable importance, and it was a large wage for that day and region. He held that post three years. After that I never heard of him any more.

WALT WITMAN

Of all nations the United States with veins full of poetical stuff most needs poets and will doubtless have the greatest and use them the greatest. Their Presidents shall not be their common referee so much as their poets shall. Of all mankind the great poet is the equable man.

The known universe has one complete lover and that is the greatest poet.... Nothing can jar him.... suffering and darkness cannot — death and fear cannot.... The great poet does not moralize or make applications of morals... he knows the soul. The soul has that measureless pride which consists in never acknowledging any lessons but its own. But it has sympathy as measureless as its pride, and the one balances the other, and neither can stretch too far while it stretches in company with the other. The inmost secrets of art sleep with the twain. The great poet has lain close betwixt both, and they are vital in his style and thoughts.

The art of art, the glory of expression and the sunshine of the light of letters is simplicity; nothing is better than simplicity.... Nothing can make up for excess or for the lack of definiteness. To carry on the heave of impulse and pierce intellectual depths and give all subjects their articulations are powers neither common nor uncommon. But to speak in literature with the perfect rectitude and insouciance of the movement of animals and the unimpeachableness of the sentiment of trees in the woods and grass by the roadside is the flawless triumph of art.

Most works are most beautiful without ornament.

... The proof of a poet is that his country absorbs him as affectionately as he has absorbed it.

Preface to November Boughs, 1888 — A Backward Glance O'er Travel'd Roads.

... I look upon Leaves of Grass, now finish'd to the end of its opportunities and powers, as my definitive *carte visite* to the coming generations of the New World, if I may assume to say so.

... Along in my sixteenth year, I had become the possessor of a stout, well-cramm'd one-thousand-page octavo volume (I have it yet) containing Walter Scott's poetry entire — an inexhaustible mine and treasury of poetic forage (especially the endless forests and jungles of notes) — has been so to me for fifty years, and remains so to this day.[1]

---

[1] Sir Walter Scott's Complete Poems; especially including Border Minstrelsy; then Sir Tristram; Lay of the Last Minstrel; Ballads from the German; Marmion; Lady of the Lake; Vision of Don Roderick; Lord of the Isles; Rokeby; Bridal of Triermain; Field of Waterloo; Harold the Dauntless; all

The chief trait of any given poet is always the spirit he brings to the observation of Humanity and Nature — the mood out of which he contemplates his subjects.

... In the free evening of my day I give to you, reader, the foregoing, garrulous talk, thoughts, reminiscences,

> As idly drifting down the ebb,
> Such ripples, half-caught voices, echo from the shore.

Concluding with two items for the imaginative genius of the West, when it worthily rises — First, what Herder taught to the young Goethe, that really great poetry is always (like the Homeric or Biblical canticles) the result of a national spirit, and not the privilege of a polish'd and select few; second, that the strongest and sweetest songs yet remain to be sung.

the dramas; various introductions; endless interesting notes and essays on Poetry, Romance, etc. (Lockhart's 1833 (or '34) edition with Scott's latest and copious revisions and annotations. All the poems were thoroughly read by me, but the ballads of the Border Minstrelsy over and over again.)

BRITISH WRITERS
JOSEPH ADDISON

The mind that lies fallow but a single day sprouts up in follies that are only to be killed by a constant and assiduous culture. It was said of Socrates, that he brought philosophy down from heaven, to inhabit among men; and I shall be ambitious to have it said of me, that I have brought philosophy out of closets and libraries, schools and colleges, to dwell in clubs and assemblies, at tea-tables and in coffee-houses.

I know several of my friends and well-wishers are in great pain for me, lest I should not be able to keep up the spirit of a paper which I oblige myself to furnish every day: but to make them easy in this particular, I will promise them faithfully to give it over as soon as I grow dull. This I know will be matter of great raillery to the small wits; who will frequently put me in mind of my promise, desire me to keep my word, assure me that it is high time to give over, with many other little pleasantries of the like nature, which men of a little smart genius cannot forbear throwing out against their best friends, when they have such a handle given them of being witty. But let them remember that I do hereby enter my caveat against this piece of raillery.

Among all kinds of writing, there is none in which authors are more apt to miscarry than in works of humor, as there is none in which they are more ambitious to excel. It is not an imagination that teems with monsters, an head that is filled with extravagant conceptions, which is capable of furnishing the world with diversions of this nature; and yet if we look into the productions of several writers, who set up men of humor, what wild irregular fancies, what unnatural distortions of thought, do we meet with? If they speak nonsense, they believe they are talking humor; and when they have drawn together a scheme of absurd inconsistent ideas, they are not able to read it over to themselves without laughing. These poor gentlemen endeavor to gain themselves the reputation of wits and humorists, by such monstrous conceits as almost qualify them for Bedlam; not considering that humor should always lie under the check of reason, and that it requires the direction of the nicest judgment, by so much the more as it indulges itself in the most boundless freedoms. There is a kind of nature that is to be observed in this sort of compositions, as well as in all other; and a certain regularity of thought which must discover the writer to be a man of sense, at the same time that he appears altogether given up to caprice. For my part, when I read the delirious mirth of an unskilful author, I cannot be so barbarous as to divert myself with it, but am rather apt to pity the man, than to laugh at anything he writes.

Aristotle has observed that ordinary writers in tragedy endeavor to raise terror and pity in their audience, not by proper sentiments and expressions, but by the dresses and decorations of the stage. There is something of this kind very ridiculous in the English theater. When the author has a mind to terrify us, it thunders; when he would make us melancholy, the stage is darkened. But among all our tragic artifices, I am the most offended at those which are made use of to inspire us with magnificent ideas of the persons that speak.

A good poet will give the reader a more lively idea of an army or a battle in a description, than if he actually saw them drawn up in squadrons and battalions, or engaged in the confusion of a fight. Our minds should be opened to great conceptions, and inflamed with glorious sentiments, by what the actor speaks, more than by what he appears. Can all the trappings or equipage of a king or hero give Brutus half that pomp and majesty which he receives from a few lines in Shakespeare?

A writer who makes fame the chief end of his endeavors, and would be more desirous of pleasing than of improving his readers, might find an inexhaustible fund of mirth in politics. Scandal and satire are never-failing gratifications to the public. Detraction and obloquy are received with as much eagerness as wit and humor.

Should a writer single out particular persons, or point his raillery at any order of men, who by their profession ought to be exempt from it; should he slander the innocent, or satirize the miserable; or should he, even on the proper subjects of derision, give the full play to his mirth, without regard to decency and good manners; he might be sure of pleasing a great part of his readers, but must be a very ill man, if by such a proceeding he could please himself.

WILLIAM BLAKE

ON HOMER'S POETRY

Every Poem must necessarily be a perfect Unity, but why Homer's is peculiarly so, I cannot tell; he has told the story of Bellerophon & omitted the Judgment of Paris, which is not only a part, but a principal part, of Homer's subject.

But when a Work has Unity, it is as much in a Part as in the Whole: the Torso is as much a Unity as the Laocoön.

As Unity is the cloke of folly, so Goodness is the cloke of knavery. Those who will have Unity exclusively in Homer come out with a Moral like a sting in the tail. Aristotle says Characters are either Good or Bad; now Goodness or Badness has nothing to do with Character: an Apple tree, a Pear tree, a Horse, a Lion are Characters, but a Good Apple tree or a Bad is an Apple tree still; a Horse is not more a Lion for being a Bad Horse: that is its Character: its Goodness or Badness is another consideration.

It is the same with the Moral of a whole Poem as with the Moral Goodness of its parts. Unity & Morality are secondary considerations, & belong to Philosophy & not to Poetry, to Exception & not to Rule, to Accident & not to Substance; the Ancients call'd it eating of the tree of good & evil.

The Classics! it is the Classics, & not Goths nor Monks, that Desolate Europe with Wars.

ON VIRGIL

Sacred Truth has pronounced that Greece & Rome, as Babylon & Egypt, so far from being parents of Arts & Sciences as they pretend, were destroyers of all Art. Homer, Virgil & Ovid confirm this opinion & make us reverence The Word of God, the only light of antiquity that remains unperverted by War. Virgil in the Æneid, Book vi, line 848, says 'Let others study Art: Rome has somewhat better to do, namely War & Dominion.'

Rome & Greece swept Art into their maw & destroy'd it; a Warlike State never can produce Art. It will Rob & Plunder & accumulate into one place, & Translate & Copy & Buy & Sell & Criticise, but not Make. Grecian is Mathematic Form: Gothic is Living Form. Mathematic Form is Eternal in the Reasoning Memory: Living Form is Eternal Existence.

JAMES BOSWELL

Had Dr. Johnson written his own life, in conformity with the opinion which he has given, that every man's life may be best written by himself; had he employed in the preservation of his own history that clearness of narration and elegance of language in which he has embalmed so many eminent persons, the world would probably have had the most perfect example of biography that was ever exhibited. But although he at different times, in a desultory manner, committed to writing many particulars of the progress of his mind and fortunes, he never had persevering diligence enough to form them into a regular composition....

As I had the honour and happiness of enjoying his friendship for upwards of twenty years; as I had the scheme of writing his life constantly in view; as he was well apprised of this circumstance, and from time to time obligingly satisfied my inquiries, by communicating to me the incidents of his early years; as I acquired a facility in recollecting, and was very assiduous in recording his conversation, of which the extraordinary vigour and vivacity constituted one of the first features of his character; and as I have spared no pains in obtaining materials concerning him, from every quarter where I could discover that they were to be found, and have been favoured with the most liberal communications by his friends; I flatter myself that few biographers have entered upon such a work as this, with more advantages; independent of literary abilities, in which I am not vain enough to compare myself with some great names who have gone before me in this kind of writing.

Instead of melting down my materials into one mass, and constantly speaking in my own person, by which I might have appeared to have more merit in the execution of the work, I have resolved to adopt and enlarge upon the excellent plan of Mr. Mason, in his Memoirs of Gray. Wherever narrative is necessary to explain, connect, and supply, I furnish it to the best of my abilities; but in the chronological series of Johnson's life, which I trace as distinctly as I can, year by year, I produce, wherever it is in my power, his own minutes, letters or conversation, being convinced that this mode is more lively, and will make my readers better acquainted with him, than even most of those were who actually knew him, but could know him only partially; whereas there is here an accumulation of intelligence from various points, by which his character is more fully understood and illustrated.

Indeed I cannot conceive a more perfect mode of writing any man's life, than not only relating all the most important events of it in their order, but interweaving what he privately wrote, and said, and thought; by which mankind are enabled as it were to see him live, and to 'live o'er each scene' with him, as he actually advanced through the several stages of his life. Had his other friends been as diligent and ardent as I was, he might have been almost entirely preserved. As it is, I will venture to say that he will be seen in this work more completely than any man who has ever yet lived.

And he will be seen as he really was; for I profess to write, not his panegyrick, which must be all praise, but his Life; which, great and good as he was, must not be supposed to be entirely perfect. To be as he was, is indeed subject of panegyrick enough to any man in this state of being; but in every picture there should be shade as well as light, and when I delineate him without reserve, I do what he himself recommended, both by his precept and his example.

... I remain firm and confident in my opinion, that minute particulars are frequently characteristick, and always amusing, when they relate to a distinguished man. I am therefore exceedingly unwilling that any thing, however slight, which my illustrious friend thought it worth his while to express, with any degree of point, should perish.

Of one thing I am certain, that, considering how highly the small portion which we have of the table-talk and other anecdotes of our celebrated writers is valued, and how earnestly it is regretted that we have not more, I am justified in preserving rather too many of Johnson's sayings, than too few; especially as from the diversity of dispositions it cannot be known with certainty beforehand, whether what may seem trifling to some, and perhaps to the collector himself, may not be most agreeable to many; and the greater number that an author can please in any degree, the more pleasure does there arise to a benevolent mind.

CHARLOTTE BRONTË

One day in the autumn of 1845 I accidentally lighted on a MS. volume of verse in my sister Emily's handwriting. Of course I was not surprised, knowing that she could and did write verse. I looked it over, and something more than surprise seized me — a deep conviction that these were not common effusions, nor at all like the poetry women generally write. I thought them condensed and terse, vigorous and genuine. To my ear they had also a peculiar music, wild, melancholy, and elevating. My sister Emily was not a person of demonstrative character, nor one on the recesses of whose mind and feelings even those nearest and dearest to her could, with impunity, intrude unlicensed: it took hours to reconcile her to the discovery I had made, and days to persuade her that such poems merited publication.... Meantime my younger sister quietly produced some of her own compositions, intimating that since Emily's had given me pleasure I might like to look at hers. I could not but be a partial judge, yet I thought that these verses too had a sweet, sincere pathos of their own. We had very early cherished the dream of one day being authors.... We agreed to arrange a small selection of our poems, and, if possible, get them printed. Averse to personal publicity, we veiled our own names under those of Currer, Ellis, and Acton Bell;[1] the ambiguous choice being dictated by a sort of conscientious scruple at as-

[1] *Poems by Currer, Ellis, and Acton Bell*. London: Aylott and Jones, 8 Paternoster Row. 1846.

suming Christian names positively masculine, while we did not like to declare ourselves women, because — without at the time suspecting that our mode of writing and thinking was not what is called 'feminine' — we had a vague impression that authoresses are liable to be looked on with prejudice; we noticed how critics sometimes used for their chastisement the weapon of personality, and for their reward a flattery which is not true praise. The bringing out of our little book was hard work. As was to be expected, neither we nor our poems were at all wanted; but for this we had been prepared at the outset; though inexperienced ourselves, we had read of the experience of others. The great puzzle lay in the difficulty of getting answers of any kind from the publishers to whom we applied. Being greatly harassed by this obstacle, I ventured to apply to Messrs. Chambers of Edinburgh for a word of advice; *they* may have forgotten the circumstance, but *I* have not, for from them I received a brief and business-like, but civil and sensible reply, on which we acted, and at last made way.

EMILY BRONTË

To Ellen Nussey

... You ask me to recommend some books for your perusal. I will do so in as few words as I can. If you like poetry let it be first-rate; Milton, Shakespeare, Thomson, Goldsmith, Pope (if you will, though I don't admire him), Scott, Byron, Campbell, Wordsworth, and Southey. Now don't be startled at the names of Shakespeare and Byron. Both these were great men, and their works are like themselves. You know how to choose the good and avoid the evil; the finest passages are always the purest, the bad are invariably revolting; you will never wish to read them over twice. Omit the comedies of Shakespeare and the *Don Juan*, perhaps the *Cain* of Byron, though the latter is a magnificent poem, and read the rest fearlessly; that must indeed be a depraved mind which can gather evil from *Henry VIII*, *Richard III*, from *Macbeth*, and *Hamlet*, and *Julius Cæsar*. Scott's sweet, wild, romantic poetry can do you no harm. Nor can Wordsworth's, nor Campbell's, nor Southey's — the greatest part at least of his; some is certainly objectionable. For history, read Hume, Rollin, and the *Universal History*, if you *can*: I never did. For fiction, read Scott alone; all novels after his are worthless. For biography, read Johnson's *Lives of the Poets*, Boswell's *Life of Johnson*, Southey's *Life of Nelson*, Lockhart's *Life of Burns*, Moore's *Life of Sheridan*, Moore's *Life of Byron*, Wolfe's *Remains*. For natural history, read Bewick, and Audubon, and Goldsmith, and White's *History of Selborne*.

To William Wordsworth

Authors are generally very tenacious of their productions, but I am not so much attached to this but that I can give it up without much distress. No doubt, if I had gone on, I should have made quite a Richardsonian concern of it.... I had materials in my head for half-a-dozen volumes.... Of course it is with considerable regret I relinquish any scheme so charming as the one I have sketched. It is very edifying and profitable to create a world out of your own brains, and people it with inhabitants, who are so many Melchisedecs, and have no father nor mother but your own imagination.

To Ellen Nussey

... If I could I would always work in silence and obscurity, and let my efforts be known by their results.

ELIZABETH BARRETT BROWNING
NOTES ON HER FUTURE HUSBAND'S WORK

A SOUL'S TRAGEDY

One who don't forego —
The after-battle work —

Strictly speaking, is not 'doesn't' the right abbreviation for only the third person? I don't — he doesn't. 'Who won't go' you might say with accuracy, perhaps.

'Who's me' — it sounds awkward — 'what's I?' Yet I doubt altogether what fine part of the dialogue all this is. Would 'what's me' sound less awkward?

'What's me' — 'it's man in me.' Yes, I think it should be 'what': For the relation of the 'it' afterwards.

> Wast not enough that I must strive, I said,
> To grow so far familiar with all you
> As find and take some way to get you — which
> To do, an age seemed far too little.

There is something obscure, as it strikes me, in the expression of this. 'As to find' seems necessary to the construction. But 'all you' (besides) appears to lead the thought from Eulalia, and you mean Eulalia — I think. The reader will doubt here, and have first and second thoughts.

> Nor missed a cloak from wardrobe, nor a dish from table.

Why such a dragging line just here? An oversight, probably. The second 'nor a' might drop out to advantage.

THE BOY AND THE ANGEL

> Morning, noon, eve and night.

Do you prefer this to

> Morning, Evening, noon and night —

for rhythm, I mean?

> As if thy voice to-day.

I think you must have meant to write

> As well as if thy voice to-day.

Not that the short lines are not good in their *places*.

> In heaven God said 'nor day nor night
> Brings one voice of my delight.'

Taking this verse with the context, will you consider if 'God said in heaven' is not of a simple and rather solemner intonation? The next line I do not like much. It might be more definite in meaning, I think.

> Entered the empty cell
> And played the craftsman well

Do you prefer to have short lines in this place, and why?

> Then forth sprang Gabriel's wings, off fell
> The flesh, remained the cell.

Is not something wrong here? If you mean that the flesh remained in the cell (named before), you do not say; and what else is said?

> To the east with prayer he turned:
> And in the angel burned.

I like and see plainly this burning in of the angel upon Theocrite as he looks to the east; but I doubt whether it will be as clear to all readers, you suggest it so very barely. Would not a touch or two improve the revelation? Do think.

> Be again the boy all curled.

At any rate you will write 'be then again'... will you not? But I doubt about the curled boy — any one 'be-curled' may be right — but a curled boy 'tout rond' does strike me as of questionable correctness. Think, yourself. And I do ask you to think besides, whether a little dilation of the latter stanzas of this simple noble ballad would not increase the significance and effect of the whole. Readers will not see at a glance all you have cast into it, unless you make more *surface* — it is my impression, at least.

GHENT TO AIX

You have finely distanced the rider in Rookwood here — not that I should think of saying so, if we had not talked of him before. You have the very trampling and breathing of the horses all through; and the sentiment is here in its right place, through all the physical force and display. Then the difficult management of the *three* horses, of the *three* individualities; and Roland carrying the interest with him triumphantly. I know you must be proud of the poem; and nobody can forget it who has looked at it once.

Lokeren, the cocks crew and twilight seemed clear.

I doubt about 'twilight seeming clear.' Is it a happy expression? But I only *doubt*, you know. The leaping up of the sun afterward, and the cattle standing black against him, and staring through the mist at the rider, — all that, — I do not call it *picture*, because it is so much better: it is the very sun and mist and cattle themselves.

And I like the description of Roland; I like *him* — seeing him; with one sharp ear bent back and the other pricked out — it is so livingly the horse, even to me who know nothing of horses in the ordinary way of sitting down and trying to remember what I know, but who recognise this for a real horse galloping. By the way, how the 'galloping' is a good galloping word! And how you felt it, and took the effect up and dilated it by repeating it over and over in your first stanza,... doubling, folding one upon another, the hoof-treads.

> I *galloped*, Dirck *galloped*, we *galloped* all three.
> Good speed cried the watch as the east gate undrew;
> Good speed from the wall, to us galloping through.
> The gate shut the porter, the light sank to rest,
> And into the midnight we *galloped* abreast.

One query at the last stanza.

> That they saved to have drunk our duke's health in but grieved.

You mean to say... 'would have grieved'... do you not? The construction seems a little imperfect.

TIME'S REVENGES

> He does though; and if some vein.

Will you consider, taking the context, whether 'he does himself' would not be better?

> If I lived to try
> I should just turn round nor ope an eye.

Do you like 'nor ope an eye'? I cannot much. Nor do I like the 'living to *try*.' You see how I tell you the truth. *My* truth. As I fancy I see the truth.

> As all my genius, all my learning
> Leave me, where there's no returning.

Is not that in the last line... somewhat weak and indefinite, for *you*?

> And purchase her the dear *invite*.

I protest zealously against that word. Now isn't it a vulgarism, and out of place altogether here? It seems to me, while I appreciate the conception of this poem fully, and much admire some things in it, that it requires more finishing than the other poems — I mean particularly the first part, but may be as wrong as possible, notwithstanding. I do beseech you in regard to all these notes to separate the right from the wrong as carefully as possible! And in the hope of your doing so, I have ventured to put down everything that came into my head.

ROBERT BURNS

The hope to be admired for ages is, in by far the greater part of those even who are authors of repute, an unsubstantial dream. For my part, my first ambition was, and still my strongest wish is, to please my compeers, the rustic inmates of the hamlet, while ever-changing language and manners shall allow me to be relished and understood. I am very willing to admit that I have some poetical abilities; and as few, if any writers, either moral or poetical, are intimately acquainted with the classes of mankind among whom I have chiefly mingled, I may have seen men and manners in a different phasis from what is common, which may assist originality of thought. Still I know very well the novelty of my character has by far the greatest share in the learned and polite notice I have lately had; and in a language where Pope and Churchill have raised the laugh, and Shenstone and Gray drawn the tear, where Thomson and Beattie have painted the landscape, and Lyttleton and Collins described the heart, I am not vain enough to hope for distinguished poetic fame.

I guess that I shall clear between two and three hundred pounds by my authorship; with that sum I intend, so far as I may be said to have any intention, to return to my old acquaintance, the plough; and, if I can meet with a lease by which I can live, to commence farmer. I do not intend to give up poetry: being bred to labour secures me independence; and the muses are my chief, sometimes have been my only enjoyment. If my practice second my resolution, I shall have principally at heart the serious business of life: but, while following my plough, or building up my shocks, I shall cast a leisure glance to that dear, that only feature of my character, which gave me the notice of my country, and the patronage of a Wallace.

Give me leave to criticise your taste in the only thing in which it is in my opinion reprehensible. You know I ought to know something of my own trade. Of pathos, sentiment, and point, you are a complete judge; but there is a quality more necessary than either, in a song, and which is the very essence of a ballad; I mean simplicity: now, if I mistake not, this last feature you are a little apt to sacrifice to the foregoing.

Ramsay, as every other poet, has not been always equally happy in his pieces; still I cannot approve of taking such liberties with an author as Mr. W. proposes doing with *The last time I came o'er the moor.* Let a poet, if he chooses, take up the idea of another, and work it into a piece of his own; but to mangle the works of the poor bard, whose tuneful tongue is now mute for ever, in the dark and narrow house; by Heaven, 'twould be sacrilege! I grant that Mr. W.'s version is an improvement; but I know Mr. W. well, and esteem him much; let him mend the song, as the Highlander mended his gun; — he gave it a new stock, a new lock, and a new barrel.

SAMUEL BUTLER

Men of the quickest apprehensions, and aptest Geniuses to anything they undertake, do not always prove the greatest Masters in it. For there is more Patience and Flegme required in those that attaine to any Degree of Perfection, then is commonly found in the Temper of active, and ready wits, that soone tire and will not hold out; as the swiftest Race-horse will not perform a longe Jorney so well as a sturdy dull Jade. Hence it is that Virgil who wanted much of that Natural easines of wit that Ovid had, did nevertheless with hard Labour and long Study in the end arrive at a higher perfection then the other with all his Dexterity of wit, but less Industry could attaine to: The same we may observe of Johnson, and Shakespeare. *For he that is able to thinke long and study well*, wil be sure to finde out better things then another man can hit upon suddenly, though of more quick and ready Parts, which is *commonly but chance, and the other Art and Judgment.*

He that would write obscure to the People neede's write nothing but plaine Reason, and Sense, then which Nothing can be more Mysterious to them. *For those to whom Mysterious things are plaine, plain Things must be mysterious.*

They that write Plays in Rime tell us that the language of Comedie ought to be common Discourse, such as men speake in familiar conversation: *as if verse were so.*

Our moderne Authors write Playes as they feed hogs in Westphalia, where but one eate's pease, or akornes, and all the rest feed upon his and one anothers excrement. So the Spaniard first invents and Designes Play's, the French borrow it from them and the English from the French.

Some writers have the unhappines, or rather Prodigious Vanity to affect an obscurity in their Stiles, indevouring by all meanes not to be understood, but rather like witches to cast a mist before the eies of their Readers. These are Owles of Athens only in avoyding the Light; which they do, not so much in regard of the Profoundnes of what they deliver, which is commonly very vulgar and slight when it is understood, but appeare's very learned, when it is disguisd in darke and insignificant expressions. To write not to be understood is no less vaine then to speake not to be heard. Fooles and Madmen use to talke to themselves in Publique, and he that publishes that which he would have no Man understand but himself do's the same thing. These are like Citizens that commonly choose the Darkest streets to set up in, or make false lights that the Spots and Steines of their Stuffs may not be perceived. But they have another Marke at which this folly always aymes, and seldom misses of, the Admiration of the weake and Ignorant, who are apt to contemne whatsoever they can understand, and admire any thing that they cannot.

There is a kind of Physiognomy in the Titles of Bookes no less then in the faces of men by which a Skilful Observer will as well know what to expect from the one as the other.

There can be nothing obscure in any Booke but by the Ignorance of the writer or the Reader. And when many Readers of excellent and known abilities concur in the Ignorance of some obscure writer, it is easy to guess on which side the fault ly's. Things of the most pure and refin'd Nature, are always most obedient to light, as glass, and Diamonds; the later of which receives a great loss from the least cloud of Foulnes, and there is no reason why it should bee otherwise in mens reason and Sense.

My writings are not set of with the Ostentation of Prologue, Epilogue nor Preface, nor Sophisticated with Songs and Dances, nor Musique nor fine women between the Cantos; Nor have any thing to commend them but the Plaine Downrightnes of the Sense.

Those who write Bookes against one another, do but Play a Prize in Defaming one another, in which nothing is to be gotten by either of them but Infamy. For as to Fence with foyles (that can do no great hurt) is an Exercise for all men of ever so great Quality to Practice; So *to play Prizes*, is only fit for meane and inferior People to use, who expose themselves to blows and wounds, for the Sport of the Rabble, only to Purchase their Approbation of their Abilities and a little Interest in their ways, and among their Parties, with the expence of their Bloud and Sometime, Lives. Those who rayle at one another in Print, encounter like the Fight of Rams, whose Hornes are but Foyles, and Rbated. And that beast that tilts with greatest Force, *gives as much of the Blow to himself, as he do's to his Enemy,* and receives as much Hurt as he gives, if their Foreheads are equally Hard, which are the only woepons that are usd by both sides (men and Beasts), in those Rancounters, and the Hardest has always the Oddes.

LORD BYRON

To John Murray

So you and Mr. Foscolo [an Italian patriot and poet settled in London, contributor to the *Quarterly*], etc., want me to undertake what you call a 'great work'? an Epic poem, I suppose, or some such pyramid. I'll try no such thing; I hate tasks. And then 'seven or eight years'! God send us all well this day three months, let alone years. If one's years can't be better employed than in sweating poesy, a man had better be a ditcher. And works, too! — is *Childe Harold* nothing? You have so many '*divine*' poems, is it nothing to have written a *Human* one? without any of your worn-out machinery.

Why, man, I could have spun the thoughts of the four cantos of that poem into twenty, had I wanted to bookmake, and its passion into as many modern tragedies. Since you want *length*, you shall have enough of *Juan*, for I'll make 50 cantos.... I mean to write my best work in *Italian*, and it will take me nine years more thoroughly to master the language; and then if my fancy exist, and I exist too, I will try what I *can* do *really*.... Neither will I make 'Ladies books' *al dillettar le femine e la plebe*. I have written from the fulness of my mind, from passion, from impulse, from many motives, but not for their 'sweet voices.' I know the precise worth of popular applause, for few Scribblers have had more of it; and if I chose to swerve into their paths, I could retain it, or resume it, or increase it. But I neither love ye, nor fear ye; and though I buy with ye and sell with ye, and talk with ye, I will neither eat with ye, drink with ye, nor pray with ye.

To John Murray

You say that *one half* [*of Don Juan*] is very good: you are *wrong*; for, if it were, it would be the finest poem in existence. *Where* is the poetry of which *one half* is good? is it the *Æneid*? is it *Milton's*? is it *Dryden's*? is it any one's except *Pope's* and *Goldsmith's*, of which *all* is good? and yet these two last are the poets your pond poets would explode. But if *one half* of the two Cantos [i.e. 3rd and 4th] be good in your opinion, what the devil would you have more? No — no; no poetry is *generally* good — only by fits and starts — and you are lucky to get a sparkle here and there. You might as well want a Midnight *all stars* as rhyme all perfect.

To John Murray

With regard to what you say of retouching the *Juans* and the *Hints*, it is all very well; but I can't *furbish*. I am like the tyger (in poesy), if I miss my first Spring, I go growling back to my Jungle. There is no second. I can't correct; I can't, and I won't. Nobody ever succeeds in it, great or small. Tasso remade the whole of his *Jerusalem*; but who ever reads that version? All the world goes to the first. Pope *added* to the *Rape of the Lock*, but did not reduce it. You must take my things as they happen to be: if they are not likely to suit, reduce their *estimate* then accordingly. I would rather give them away than hack and hew them. I don't say that you are not right: I merely assert that I cannot better them. I must either 'make a spoon, or spoil a horn.' And there's an end.

To Isaac Disraeli

I really cannot know whether I am or am not the Genius you are pleased to call me, but I am very willing to put up with the mistake, if it be one. It is a title dearly enough bought by most men, to render it endurable, even when not quite clearly made out, which it never *can* be till the Posterity, whose decisions are merely dreams to ourselves, has sanctioned or denied it, while it can touch us no further.... If there are any questions which you would like to ask me as connected with your Philosophy of the literary Mind (*if* mine be a literary mind), I will answer them fairly or give a reason for *not* — good, bad, or indifferent. At present I am paying the penalty of having helped to spoil the public taste, for, as long as I wrote in the false exaggerated style of youth and the times in which we live, they applauded me to the very echo; and within these few years, when I have endeavoured at better things and written what I suspect to have the principle of duration in it, the Church, the Chancellor, and all men — even to my grand patron, Francis Jeffrey, Esqre., of the *E.R.* — have risen up against me and my later publications. Such is Truth! Men dare not look her in the face, except by degrees: they mistake her for a Gorgon, instead of knowing her to be a Minerva.

To John Hamilton Reynolds

The first thing a young writer must expect, and yet can least of all suffer, is *criticism*. I did not bear it — a few years, and many changes have since passed over my head, and my reflections on that subject are attended with regret. I find, dispassionate comparison, my own revenge more than the provocation warranted. It is true, I was very young, — that might be an excuse to those I attacked — but to *me* it is none. The best reply to all objections is to write better, and if your enemies will not then do you justice, the world will. On the other hand, you should not be discouraged; to be opposed is not to be vanquished, though a timid mind is apt to mistake every scratch for a mortal wound. There is a saying of Dr. Johnson's, which it is as well to remember, that 'no man was ever written down except by himself.' I hope you will meet with as few obstacles as yourself can desire; but if you should, you will find that they are to be *stepped* over; to *kick* them down is the first resolve of a young and fiery spirit, a pleasant thing enough at the time, but not so afterwards: on this point, I speak of a man's *own* reflections; what others think or say is a *secondary* consideration, at least, it has been so with me, but will not answer as a general maxim: he who would make his way in the world must let the world believe that it was made for him, and accommodate himself to the minutest observance of its regulations.

To Percy Bysshe Shelley

I am very sorry to hear what you say of Keats — is it *actually* true? I did not think criticism had been so killing. Though I differ from you essentially in your estimate of his performances, I so much abhor all unnecessary pain, that I would rather he had been seated on the highest peak of Parnassus than have perished in such a manner. Poor fellow! though with such inordinate self-love he would probably have not been very happy. I read the review of *Endymion* in the *Quarterly*. It was severe, — but surely not so severe as many reviews in that and other journals upon others. I recollect the effect on me of the *Edinburgh* on my first poem; it was rage, and resistance, and redress — but not despondency nor despair. I grant that those are not amiable feelings; but in this world of bustle and broil, and especially in the career of writing, a man should calculate on his powers of *resistance* before he goes into the arena.

> Expect not life from pain nor danger free,
> Nor deem the doom of man reversed for thee.

... I have published a pamphlet on the Pope controversy, which you will not like. Had I known that Keats was dead — or that he was alive and so sensitive — I should have omitted some remarks upon his poetry, to which I was provoked by his *attack* upon *Pope*, and my disapprobation of *his own* style of writing.

To John Murray

Is it true, what Shelley writes me, that poor John Keats died at Rome of the *Quarterly Review*? I am very sorry for it.... I know, by experience, that a savage review is Hemlock to a sucking author; and the one on me (which produced the *English Bards*, *etc.*), knocked me down — but I got up again. Instead of bursting a blood-vessel, I drank three bottles of Claret, and began an answer, finding that there was nothing in the Article for which I could lawfully knock Jeffrey on the head, in an honourable way. However, I would not be the person who wrote the homicidal article, for all the honour and glory in the World, though I by no means approve of that School of Scribbling which it treats upon.

To Thomas Moore

The truth is, my dear Moore, you live near the *stove* of society, where you are unavoidably influenced by its heat and its vapours. I did so once — and too much — and enough to give a colour to my whole future existence. As my success in society was *not* inconsiderable, I am surely not a prejudiced judge upon the subject, unless in its favour; but I think it, as now constituted, *fatal* to all great original undertakings of every kind. I never courted it *then*, when I was young and high in blood, and one of its 'curled darlings'; and do you think I would do so *now*, when I am living in a clearer atmosphere? One thing *only* might lead me back to it, and that is, to try once more if I could do any good in *politics*; but *not* in the petty politics I see now preying upon our miserable country.

Do not let me be misunderstood, however. If you speak your *own* opinions, they ever had, and will have, the greatest weight with *me*. But if you merely *echo* the *monde* (and it is difficult not to do so, being in its favour and its ferment), I can only regret that you should ever repeat any thing to which I cannot pay attention.

To Thomas Moore

You say the *Doge* will not be popular: did I ever write for *popularity*? I defy you to show a work of mine (except a tale or two) of a popular style or complexion. It appears to me that there is room for a different style of the drama; neither a servile following of the old drama, which is a grossly erroneous one, nor yet *too French*, like those who succeeded the older writers. It appears to me, that good English, and a severer approach to the rules, might combine something not dishonourable to our literature. I have also attempted to make a play without love; and there are neither rings, nor mistakes, nor starts, nor outrageous ranting villains, nor melodrama in it. All this will prevent its popularity, but does not persuade me that it is *therefore* faulty. Whatever faults it has will arise from deficiency in the conduct, rather than in the conception, which is simple and severe.

To Mr. Perry

Ravenna, January 22, 1821

Dear Sir, I have received a strange piece of news, which cannot be more disagreeable to your public than it is to me. Letters and the gazettes do me the honour to say that it is the intention of some of the London managers to bring forward on their stage the poem of *marino Faliero*, &c. which was never intended for such an exhibition, and I trust will never undergo it. It is certainly unfit for it. I have never written but for the solitary *reader*, and require no experiments for applause beyond his silent approbation. Since such an attempt to drag me forth as a gladiator in the theatrical arena is a violation of all the courtesies of literature, I trust that the impartial part of the press will step between me and this pollution. I say pollution, because every violation of a *right* is such, and I claim my right as an author to prevent what I have written from being turned into a stage-play. I have too much respect for the public to permit this of my own free will. Had I sought their favour, it would have been by a pantomime.

... In my mind, the highest of all poetry is ethical poetry, as the highest of all earthly objects must be moral truth. Religion does not make a part of my subject; it is something beyond human powers, and has failed in all human hands except Milton's and Dante's, and even Dante's powers are involved in his delineation of human passions, though in supernatural circumstances. What made Socrates the greatest of men? His moral truth — his ethics. What proved Jesus Christ the Son of God hardly less than his miracles? His moral precepts. And if ethics have made a philosopher the first of men, and have not been disdained as an adjunct to his Gospel by the Deity himself, are we to be told that ethical poetry, or didactic poetry, or by whatever name you term it, whose object is to make men better and wiser, is not the *very first order* of poetry; and are we to be told this too by one of the priesthood? It requires more mind, more wisdom, more power, than all the 'forests' that ever were 'walked' for their 'description,' and all the epics that ever were founded upon fields of battle. The *Georgics* are indisputably, and, I believe, *undisputedly* even a finer poem than the *Æneid*. Virgil knew this; he did not order *them* to be burnt.

The proper study of mankind is man.

It is the fashion of the day to lay great stress upon what they call 'imagination' and 'invention,' the two commonest of qualities: an Irish peasant with a little whiskey in his head will imagine and invent more than would furnish forth a modern poem. If Lucretius had not been spoiled by the Epicurean system, we should have had a far superior poem to any now in existence. As mere poetry, it is the first of Latin poems. What then has ruined it? His ethics. Pope has not this defect; his moral is as pure as his poetry is glorious.

SAMUEL TAYLOR COLERIDGE

During the first year that Mr. Wordsworth and I were neighbours, our conversations turned frequently on the two cardinal points of poetry, the power of exciting the sympathy of the reader by a faithful adherence to the truth of nature, and the power of giving the interest of novelty by the modifying colours of imagination. The sudden charm which accidents of light and shade, which moonlight or sunset, diffused over a known and familiar landscape appeared to represent the practicability of combining both. These are the poetry of nature. The thought suggested itself (to which of us I do not recollect) that a series of poems might be composed of two sorts. In the one, the incidents and agents were to be, in part at least, supernatural; and the excellence aimed at was to consist in the interesting of the affections by the dramatic truth of such emotions as would naturally accompany such situations, supposing them real. And real in this sense they have been to every human being who, from whatever source of delusion, has at any time believed himself under supernatural agency. For the second class, subjects were to be chosen from ordinary life; the characters and incidents were to be such as will be found in every village and its vicinity where there is meditative and feeling mind to seek after them, or to notice them when they present themselves.

In this idea originated the plan of the Lyrical Ballads; in which it was agreed that my endeavours should be directed to persons and characters supernatural, or at least romantic; yet so as to transfer from our inward nature a human interest and a semblance of truth sufficient to procure for these shadows of imagination that willing suspension of disbelief for the moment, which constitutes poetic faith. Mr. Wordsworth, on the charm of novelty to things of every day, and to excite a feeling analogous to the supernatural, by awakening the mind's attention from the lethargy of custom, and directing it to the loveliness and the wonders of the world before us; an inexhaustible treasure, but for which, in consequence of the film of familiarity and selfish solicitate, we have eyes, yet see not, ears that hear not, and hearts that neither feel nor understand.

With this view I wrote the Ancient Mariner, and was preparing among other poems, the Dark Ladie, and the Christabel, in which I should have more nearly realised my ideal than I had done in my first attempt. But Mr. Wordsworth's industry had proved so much more successful, and the number of his poems so much greater, that my compositions, instead of forming a balance, appeared rather an interpolation of heterogeneous matter. Mr. Wordsworth added two or three poems written in his own character, in the impassioned, lofty, and sustained diction which is characteristic of his genius. In this form the Lyrical Ballads were published; and were presented by him as an experiment, whether subjects, which from their nature rejected the usual ornaments and extra-colloquial style of poems in general, might not be so managed in the language of ordinary life as to produce the pleasurable interest which it is the peculiar business of poetry to impart.

JOSEPH CONRAD

[The following words are addressed to Edward Garnett:]

You no doubt have the gift of the 'mot juste,' of those sentences that are like a flash of limelight on the façade of a cathedral or a flash of lightning on a landscape when the whole scene and all the details leap up before the eye in a moment and are irresistibly impressed on memory by their sudden vividness.

Since I sent you that part 1st (on the eleventh of the month) I have written one page. Just one page. I went about thinking and forgetting — sitting down before the blank page to find that I could not put one sentence together. To be able to think and unable to express is a fine torture. I am undergoing it — without patience. I don't see the end of it. It's very ridiculous and very awful. Now I've got all my people together I don't know what to do with them. The progressive episodes of the story *will* not emerge from the chaos of my sensations. I feel nothing clearly. And I am frightened when I remember that I have to drag it all out of myself.

Other writers have some starting point. Something to catch hold of. They start from an anecdote — from a newspaper paragraph (a book may be suggested by a casual sentence in an old almanack). They lean on dialect — or on tradition — or on history — or on the prejudice or fad of the hour; they trade upon some tie or some conviction of their time — or upon the absence of these things — which they can abuse or praise. But at any rate they know something to begin with — while I don't. I have had some impressions, some sensations — in my time: — impressions and sensations of common things. And it's all faded — my very being seems faded and thin like the ghost of a blonde and sentimental woman, haunting romantic ruins pervaded by rats. I am exceedingly miserable. My task appears to me as sensible as lifting the world without that fulcrum which even that conceited ass, Archimedes, admitted to be necessary.

You are right in your criticism of *Outpost*. The construction is bad. It is bad because it was a matter of conscious decision, and I have no discrimination — in artistic sense. Things get themselves written — and you like them. Things get themselves into shape — and they are tolerable. But when I want to write — when I do consciously try to write or try to construct, then my ignorance has full play and the quality of my miserable and benighted intelligence is disclosed to the scandalized gaze of my literary father. This is as it should be. I always told you I was a kind of inspired humbug. Now you know it. Let me assure you that your remarks were a complete disclosure to me. I had not the slightest glimmer of my stupidity. I am now profoundly thankful to find I have enough sense to see the truth of what you say. It's very evident that the first 3 pages kill all the interest. And I wrote them of set purpose!! I thought I was achieving artistic simplicity!!!!!! Now, of course, the thing — the *res infecta* — is as plain as a pikestaff. It does not improve my opinion of myself and of my prospects. Am I totally lost? Or do the last few pages save the thing from being utterly contemptible? You seem to think so — if I read your most kind and friendly letter aright.

I must explain that that particular story was no more meant for you than the *Idiots* — that is, *all* the short stories (*ab initio*) were *meant alike* for a vol. to be inscribed to *you*. Only then I had not heard from you so long that you were naturally constantly in my thoughts. In fact I worried about it, thinking of the treachery of disease and so on. And then I thought that the story would be a good title-story — better than the *Idiots*. It would sound funny, a title like this: *Idiots and other Stories*. While *Outpost of Progress and Other Stories sounds* nice and proper.

THE ART OF THE TRANSLATOR

Tuesday
(December 7, 1897)

Dearest Garnett

Thanks. It is admirable — admirable. I am not speaking of Turgeniev. But surely to render thus the very spirit of an incomparable artist one must have more than a spark of the sacred fire. The reader does not *see* the language — the story is alive — as living as when it came from the master's hand. This is a great achievement. I have been reading with inexpressible delight — not the delight of novelty, for I knew and remembered the stories before — but with the delight of reveling in that pellucid flaming atmosphere of Turgeniev's life which the translator has preserved unstained, unchilled, with the clearness and heat of original inspiration. To me there is something touching like a great act of self-sacrifice and devotion in this perfect fidelity to a departed breath. The capacity to be so true to what is best is a great — an incomparable gift.

Dearest Edward

The trouble is that I too don't know Russian; I don't even know the alphabet. The truth of the matter is that it is *you* who have opened my eyes to the value and the quality of Turgeniev. As a boy I remember reading Smoke in a Polish translation (a *feuilleton* of some newspaper) and the Gentlefolks in French. I liked those things purely by instinct (a very sound ground but not starting point for criticism) with which the consciousness of literary perfection had absolutely nothing to do. You opened my mind first to the appreciation of the art. For the rest Turgeniev for me is Constance Garnett and Constance Garnett *is* Turgeniev. She has done that marvelous thing of placing the man's work inside English literature and it is there that I see it — or rather that I *feel* it.

Upon the whole I don't see it. If I did see I could talk about it, perhaps to some purpose. As it is, my dear, I wouldn't know how to begin.

As far as I know you are the only man who had seen T not only in his relation to mankind but in his relation to Russia. And he is great in both. But to be so great and at the same time so fine is fatal to an artist — as to any other man for that matter. It isn't Dostoevsky the grimacing haunted creature who is under a curse; it is Turgeniev. Every gift has been heaped on his cradle. Absolute sanity and the deepest sensibility, the clearest vision and the most exquisite responsiveness, penetrating insight for the significant, for the essential in human life and in the visible world, the clearest mind, the warmest heart, the largest sympathy — and all that in perfect measure! There's enough there to ruin any writer. For you know, my dear Edward, that if you and I were to catch Antinous and exhibit him in a booth of the world's fair, swearing that his life was as perfect as his form, we wouldn't get one per cent. of the crowd struggling next door to catch the sight of the double-headed Nightingale or of some weak-kneed giant grinning through a collar.

CHARLES DICKENS

But the story contains admirable writing, and many clear evidences of a very delicate discrimination of character. It is delightful to find throughout that you have taken great pains with it besides, and have 'gone at it' with a perfect knowledge of the jolter-headedness of the conceited idiots who suppose that volumes are to be tossed off like pancakes, and that any writing can be done without the utmost application, the greatest patience, and the steadiest energy of which the writer is capable.

I hold my inventive capacity on the stern condition that it must master my whole life, often have complete possession of me, make its own demands upon me, and sometimes, for months together, put everything else away from me. If I had not known long ago that my place could never be held, unless I were at any moment ready to devote myself to it entirely, I should have dropped out of it very soon. All this I can hardly expect you to understand — or the restlessness and waywardness of an author's mind.

These *Notes* are destroyed by too much smartness. It gives the appearance of perpetual effort, stabs to the heart the nature that is in them, and wearies by the manner and not by the matter. It is the commonest fault in the world (as I have constant occasion to observe here), but it is a very great one.

Again I must say, above all things — especially to young people writing: For the love of God, don't condescend!

But it strikes me that you constantly hurry your narrative (and yet without getting on) by telling it, in a sort of impetuous breathless way, in your own person, when the people should tell it and act it for themselves. My notion always is, that when I have made the people to play out the play it is, as it were, their business to do it, and not mine.

I think you are too ambitious, and that you have not sufficient knowledge of life or character to venture on so comprehensive an attempt. Evidences of inexperience in every way, and of your power being far below the situations that you imagine, present themselves to me in almost every page I have read.

I don't quite agree with you in two small respects. First, I question very much whether it would have been a good thing for every great man to have had his Boswell, inasmuch that I think that two Boswells, or three at most, would have made great men extraordinarily false, and would have set them on always playing a part, and would have made distinguished people about them for ever restless and distrustful. I can imagine a succession of Boswells bringing about a tremendous state of falsehood in society, and playing the very devil with confidence and friendship. Secondly, I cannot help objecting to that practice (begun, I think, or greatly enlarged by Hunt) of italicising lines and words and whole passages in extracts, without some very special reason indeed. It does appear to be a kind of assertion of the editor over the reader — almost over the author himself — which grates upon me. The author might almost as well do it himself to my thinking, as a disagreeable thing; and it is such a strong contrast to the modest, quiet, tranquil beauty of The Deserted Village, for instance, that I would almost as soon hear 'the town crier' speak the lines. The practice always reminds me of a man seeing a beautiful view, and not thinking how beautiful it is half so much as what he shall say about it.

BENJAMIN DISRAELI

COMPOSITION

I have observed that, after writing a book, my mind always makes a great spring. I believe that the act of composition produces the same invigorating effect upon the mind which some exertion does upon the body. Even the writing of Manstein produced a revolution in my nature, which cannot be traced by any metaphysical analysis. In the course of a few days, I was converted from a worldling into a philosopher. I was indeed ignorant, but I had lost the double ignorance of the Platonists; I was no longer ignorant that I was ignorant. No one could be influenced by a greater desire of knowledge, a greater passion for the beautiful, or a deeper regard for his fellow-creatures. And I well remember when, on the evening that I wrote the last sentence of this more intellectual effort, I walked out upon the terrace with that feeling of satisfaction which accompanies the idea of a task completed. So far was I from being excited by the hope of having written a great work, that I even meditated its destruction; for the moment it was terminated, it seemed to me that I had become suddenly acquainted with the long-concealed principles of my art, which, without doubt, had been slenderly practised in this production. My taste, as it were in an instant, became formed; and I felt convinced I could now produce some lasting creation.

I thought no more of criticism. The breath of man has never influenced me much, for I depend more upon myself than upon others. I want no false fame. It would be no delight to me to be considered a prophet, were I conscious of being an impostor. I ever wish to be undeceived; but if I possess the organization of a poet, no one can prevent me from exercising my faculty, any more than he can rob the courser of his fleetness, or the nightingale of her song.

The profound thinker always suspects that he is superficial. Patience is a necessary ingredient of genius. Nothing is more fatal than to be seduced into composition by the first flutter of the imagination. This is the cause of so many weak and unequal works, of so many worthy ideas thrown away, and so many good purposes marred. Yet there is a bound to meditation; there is a moment when further judgment is useless. There is a moment when a heavenly light rises over the dim world you have been so long creating, and bathes it with life and beauty. Accept this omen that your work is good, and revel in the sunshine of composition. — *Contarini Fleming*.

NOVEL (RECEIPT FOR WRITING A)

Take a pair of pistols and a pack of cards, a cookerybook and a set of new quadrilles; mix them up with half an intrigue and a whole marriage, and divide them into three equal portions. — *The Young Duke*.

THOMAS HARDY

(April) 15. Good Friday. Read review of Tess in *The Quarterly*. A smart and amusing article; but it is easy to be smart and amusing if a man will forgo veracity and sincerity.... How strange that one may write a book without knowing what one puts into it — or rather, the reader reads into it. Well, if this sort of thing continues no more novel-writing for me. A man must be a fool to deliberately stand up to be shot at.

July 1. We don't always remember as we should that in getting at the truth we get only at the true nature of the impression that an object, etc., produces on us, the true thing in itself being still, as Kant shows, beyond our knowledge.

The art of observation (during travel, etc.) consists in this: the seeing of great things in little things, the whole in the part — even the infinitesimal part. For instance, you are abroad: you see an English flag on a ship-mast from the window of your hotel: you realize the English navy. Or, at home, in a soldier you see the British Army, in a bishop at your club, the Church of England; and in a steam hooter you hear Industry.

October 24. The best tragedy — highest tragedy in short — is that of the WORTHY encompassed by the INEVITABLE. The tragedies of immoral and worthless people are not of the best.

February 23. A story must be exceptional enough to justify its telling. We tale-tellers are all Ancient Mariners, and none of us is warranted in stopping Wedding Guests (in other words, the hurrying public) unless he has something more unusual to relate than the ordinary experience of every average man and woman.

The whole secret of fiction and the drama — in the constructional part — lies in the adjustment of things unusual to things eternal and universal. The writer who knows exactly how exceptional, and how non-exceptional, his events should be made, possesses the key to the art.

To Swinburne

I must thank you for your kind note about my fantastic little tale (*The Well-Beloved*), which, if it can make, in its better parts, any faint claim to imaginative feeling, will owe something of such feeling to you, for I often thought of lines of yours during the writing; and indeed, was not able to resist the quotation of your words now and then.

And this reminds me that one day, when examining several English imitations of a well-known fragment of Sappho, I interested myself in trying to strike out a better equivalent for it than the commonplace 'Thou, too, shalt die,' etc., which all the translators had used during the last hundred years. I then stumbled upon your 'Thee, too, the years shall cover,' and all my spirit for poetic pains died out of me. Those few words present, I think, the finest *drama* of Death and Oblivion, so to speak, in our tongue.

There is no new poetry; but the new poet — if he carry the flame on further (and if not he is no new poet) — comes with a new note. And that new note it is that troubles the critical waters.

Poetry is emotion put into measure. The emotion must come by nature, but the measure can be acquired by art.

January (1899). No man's poetry can be truly judged till its last line is written. What is the last line? The death of the poet. And hence there is this quaint consolation to any writer of verse — that it may be imperishable for all that anybody can tell him to the contrary; and that if worthless he can never know it, unless he be a greater adept at self-criticism than poets usually are.

WILLIAM HAZLITT

Neither a mere description of natural objects, nor a mere delineation of natural feelings, however distinct or forcible, constitutes the ultimate end and aim of poetry, without the heightenings of the imagination. The light of poetry is not only a direct but also a reflected light, that while it shews us the object, throws a sparkling radiance on all around it: the flame of the passions, communicated to the imagination, reveals to us, as with a flash of lightning, the inmost recesses of thought, and penetrates our whole being. Poetry represents forms chiefly as they suggest other forms; feelings, as they suggest forms or other feelings. Poetry puts a spirit of life and motion into the universe. It describes the flowing, not the fixed. It does not define the limits of sense, or analyse the distinctions of the understanding, but signifies the excess of the imagination beyond the actual or ordinary impression of any object or feeling. The poetical impression of any object is that uneasy, exquisite sense of beauty or power that cannot be contained within itself; that is impatient of all limit; that (as flame bends to flame) strives to link itself to some other image of kindred beauty or grandeur; to enshrine itself, as it were, in the highest forms of fancy, and to relieve the aching sense of pleasure by expressing it in the boldest manner, and by the most striking examples of the same quality in other instances. Poetry, according to Lord Bacon, for this reason, 'has something divine in it, because it raises the mind and hurries it into sublimity, by conforming the shows of things to the desires of the soul, instead of subjecting the soul to external things, as reason and history do.' It is strictly the language of the imagination; and the imagination is that faculty which represents objects, not as they are in themselves, but as they are moulded by other thoughts and feelings, into an infinite variety of shapes and combinations of power.

ON FAMILIAR STYLE

It is not easy to write a familiar style. Many people mistake a familiar for a vulgar style, and suppose that to write without affectation is to write at random. On the contrary, there is nothing that requires more precision, and, if I may so say, purity of expression, than the style I am speaking of. It utterly rejects not only all unmeaning pomp, but all low, cant phrases, and loose, unconnected, *slipshod* allusions. It is not to take the first word that offers, but the best word in common use; it is not to throw words together in any combinations we please, but to follow and avail ourselves of the true idiom of the language. To write a genuine familiar or truly English style is to write as any one would speak in common conversation who had a thorough command and choice of words, or who could discourse with ease, force, and perspicuity, setting aside all pedantic and oratorical flourishes. Or to give another illustration, to write naturally is the same thing in regard to common conversation as to read naturally is in regard to common speech. It does not follow that it is an easy thing to give the true accent and inflection to the words you utter, because you do not attempt to rise above the level of ordinary life and colloquial speaking. You do not assume, indeed, the solemnity of the pulpit, or the tone of stage-declamation; neither are you at liberty to gabble on at a venture, without emphasis or discretion, or to resort to vulgar dialect or clownish pronunciation. You must steer a middle course. You are tied down to a given and appropriate articulation, which is determined by the habitual associations between sense and sound, and which you can only hit by entering into the author's meaning, as you must find the proper words and style to express yourself by fixing your thoughts on the subject you have to write about. Any one may mouth out a passage with a theatrical cadence, or get upon stilts to tell his thoughts; but to write or speak with propriety and simplicity is a more difficult task. Thus it is easy to affect a pompous style, to use a word twice as big as the thing you want to express: it is not so easy to pitch upon the very word that exactly fits it. Out of eight or ten words equally common, equally intelligible, with nearly equal pretensions, it is a matter of some nicety and discrimination to pick out the very one, the preferableness of which is scarcely perceptible, but decisive.

The proper force of words lies not in the words themselves, but in their application. A word may be a fine-sounding word, of an unusual length, and very imposing from its learning and novelty, and yet in the connection in which it is introduced may be quite pointless and irrelevant. It is not pomp or pretension, but the adaptation of the expression to the idea, that clenches a writer's meaning: — as it is not the size or glossiness of the materials, but their being fitted each to its place, that gives strength to the arch; or as the pegs and nails are as necessary to the support of the building as the larger timbers, and more so than the mere showy, unsubstantial ornaments. I hate any thing that occupies more space than it is worth. I hate to see a load of band-boxes go along the street, and I hate to see a parcel of big words without anything in them. A person who does not deliberately dispose of all his thoughts alike in cumbrous draperies and flimsy disguises may strike out twenty varieties of familiar every-day language, each coming somewhat nearer to the feeling he wants to convey, and at last not hit upon that particular and only one which may be said to be identical with the exact impression in his mind. This would seem to show that Mr. Cobbett is hardly right in saying that the first word that occurs is always the best. It may be a very good one; and yet a better may present itself on reflection or from time to time. It should be suggested naturally, however, and spontaneously, from a fresh and lively conception of the subject. We seldom succeed by trying at improvement, or by merely substituting one word for another that we are not satisfied with, as we cannot recollect the name of a place or person by merely plaguing ourselves about it. We wander farther from the point by persisting in a wrong scent; but it starts up accidentally in the memory when we least expected it, by touching some link in the chain of previous association.

LEIGH HUNT

Sitting last winter among my books, and walled round with all the comfort and protection which they and my fireside could afford me — to wit, a table of high-piled books at my back, my writing-desk on one side of me, some shelves on the other, and the feeling of the warm fire at my feet — I began to consider how I loved the authors of those books: how I loved them too, not only for the imaginative pleasures they afforded me, but for their making me love the very books themselves, and delight to be in contact with them. I looked sideways at my *Spenser*, my *Theocritus*, and my *Arabian Nights*; then above them at my Italian poets; then behind me at my *Dryden* and *Pope*, my romances, and my *Boccaccio*; then on my left side at my *Chaucer*, who lay on a writing-desk; and thought how natural it was in C. L. to give a kiss to an old folio, as I once saw him do to *Chapman's Homer*. At the same time I wondered how he could sit in that front room of his with nothing but a few unfeeling tables and chairs, or at best a few engravings in trim frames, instead of putting a couple of armchairs into the back-room with the books in it, where there is but one window. Would I were there, with both the chairs properly filled, and one or two more besides! 'We had talk, sir' — the only talk capable of making one forget the books.

I entrench myself in my books equally against sorrow and the weather. If the wind comes through a passage, I look about to see how I can fence it off by a better disposition of my movables; if a melancholy thought is importunate, I give another glance at my *Spenser*. When I speak of being in contact with my books I mean it literally. I like to lean my head against them. Living in a southern climate, though in a part sufficiently northern to feel the winter, I was obliged during that season to take some of the books out of the study, and hang them up near the fire-place in the sitting-room, which is the only room that has such a convenience. I therefore walled myself in, as well as I could, in the manner above-mentioned. I took a walk every day, to the astonishment of the Genoese, who used to huddle against a bit of sunny wall like flies on a chimney-piece; but I did this only that I might so much the more enjoy my *English* evening. The fire was a wood fire instead of a coal; but I imagined myself in the country. I remembered at the very worst, that one end of my native land was not nearer the other than England is to Italy.

While writing this article I am in my study again. Like the rooms in all the houses in this country which are not hovels, it is handsome and ornamented. On one side it looks towards a garden and the mountains; on another, to the mountains and the sea. What signifies all this? I turn my back upon the sea; I shut up even one of the side windows looking upon the mountains, and retain no prospect but that of the trees. On the right and left of me are book-shelves; a bookcase is affectionately open in front of me; and thus kindly enclosed with my books and the green leaves, I write. If all this is too luxurious and effeminate, of all luxuries it is the one that leaves you the most strength. And this is to be said for scholarship in general. It unfits a man for activity; for his bodily part in the world; but it often doubles both the power and the sense of his mental duties; and with much indignation against his body, and more against those who tyrannise over the intellectual claims of mankind, the man of letters, like the magician of old, is prepared 'to play the devil' with the great men of this world, in a style that astonishes both the sword and the toga.

I do not like this fine large study. I like elegance. I like room to breathe in, and even walk about, when I want to breathe and walk about. I like a great library next my study; but for the study itself give me a small snug place, almost entirely walled with books. There should be only one window in it, looking upon trees. Some prefer a place with few or no books at all — nothing but a chair, or a table, like Epictetus; but I should say that these were philosophers, not lovers of books; if I did not recollect that Montaigne was both. He had a study in a round tower, walled as aforesaid. It is true, one forgets one's books while writing — at least they say so. For my part, I think I have them in a sort of sidelong mind's eye; like a second thought, which is more — like a waterfall, or a whispering wind.

SAMUEL JOHNSON

Nothing can please many, and please long, but just representations of general nature. Particular manners can be known to few, and therefore few only can judge how nearly they are copied. The irregular combinations of fanciful invention may delight awhile, by that novelty of which the common satiety of life sends us all in quest; but the pleasures of sudden wonder are soon exhausted, and *the mind can only repose on the stability of truth.*

If there be, what I believe there is, in every nation, a style which never becomes obsolete, a certain mode of phraseology so consonant and congenial to the analogy and principles of its respective language as to remain settled and unaltered: this style is probably to be sought in the common intercourse of life, among those who speak only to be understood, without ambition or elegance.

The polite are always catching modish innovations, and the learned depart from established forms of speech, in hope of finding or making better; those who wish for distinction forsake the vulgar, when the vulgar is right; but there is a conversation above grossness and below refinement, where propriety resides, and where this poet seems to have gathered his comic dialogue. He is therefore more agreeable to the ears of the present age than any other author equally remote, and among his other excellencies deserves to be studied as one of the original masters of our language.

JOHN KEATS

Hampstead, 27 Feb. (1818)

My dear Taylor,

... In Endymion, I have most likely but moved into the go-cart from the leading-strings. In poetry I have a few axioms, and you will see how far I am from their centre.

1st. I think poetry should surprise by a fine excess, and not by singularity; it should strike the reader as a wording of his own highest thoughts, and appear almost a remembrance.

2nd. Its touches of beauty should never be halfway, thereby making the reader breathless, instead of content. The rise, the progress, the setting of imagery, should, like the sun, come natural to him, shine over him, and set soberly, although in magnificence, leaving him in the luxury of twilight. But it is easier to think what poetry should be, than to write it. And this leads me to

Another axiom — That, if poetry comes not as naturally as the leaves to a tree, it had better not come at all. However it may be with me, I cannot help looking into new countries with 'Oh, for a muse of fire to ascend!'

If Endymion serves me as a pioneer, perhaps I ought to be content, for, thank God, I can read, and perhaps understand, Shakespeare to his depths; and I have, I am sure, many friends, who, if I fail, will attribute any change in my life and temper to humbleness rather than pride — to a cowering under the wings of great poets, rather than to a bitterness that I am not appreciated. I am anxious to get Endymion printed that I may forget it, and proceed. I have copied the Third Book, and begun the Fourth. I will take care the printer shall not trip up my heels.

To Benjamin Bailey

I should not have consented to myself, these four months, tramping in the Highlands, but that I thought it would give me more experience, rub off more prejudice, use [me] to more hardship, identify finer scenes, load me with grander mountains, and strengthen more my reach in poetry, than would stopping at home among books, even though I should reach Homer. By this time I am comparatively a mountaineer; I have been among wilds and mountains too much to break out much about their grandeur. I have fed upon oatcake not long enough to be very much attached to it. The first mountains I saw, though not so large as some I have since seen, weighed very solemnly upon me. The effect is wearing away, yet I like them mainly. We have come this evening with a guide — for without was impossible — into the middle of the Isle of Mull, pursuing our cheap journey to Iona, and perhaps Staffa. We would not follow the common and fashionable mode, from the great imposition of expense....

You say I must study Dante: well, the only books I have with me are those three little volumes. I read that fine passage you mention a few days ago. Your letter followed me from Hampstead to Port Patrick, and thence to Glasgow. You must think me, by this time, a very pretty fellow.... Brown keeps on writing volumes of adventure to Dilke. When we get in of an evening, and I have perhaps taken my rest on a couple of chairs, he affronts my indolence and luxury, by pulling out of his knapsack, first, his paper; secondly, his pens; and lastly, his ink. Now I would not care if he would change a little. I say now, why not, Bailey, take out his pens first sometimes. But I might as well tell a hen to hold up her head before she drinks, instead of afterwards.

CHARLES LAMB

... Write — and all your friends will hate you — all will suspect you. Are you happy in drawing a character? Show it not for yours. Not one of your acquaintance but will surmise that you meant him or her — no matter how discordant from their own. Let it be diametrically different, their fancy will extract from it some lines of a likeness. I lost a friend — a most valuable one — by showing him a whimsical draught of a miser. He himself is remarkable for generosity, even to carelessness in money matters; but there was an expression in it, out of Juvenal, about an attic — a place where pigeons are fed; and my friend kept pigeons. All the waters in the Danube cannot wash it out of his pate to this day, but that in my miser I was making reflections upon *him*.

Samuel Johnson, whom, to distinguish from the doctor, we may call the Whig, was a very remarkable writer. He may be compared to his contemporary, Dr. Fox, whom he resembled in many points. He is another instance of King William's discrimination, which was so superior to that of any of his ministers. Johnson was one of the most formidable of the advocates for the Exclusion Bill; and he suffered by whipping and imprisonment under James accordingly. Like Asgill, he argues with great apparent candour and clearness till he gets his opponent within reach; and then comes a blow as from a sledge-hammer. I do not know where I could put my hand on a book containing so much sense and constitutional doctrine as this thin folio of Johnson's Works; and what party in this country would read so severe a lecture in it as our modern Whigs? A close reasoner and a good writer in general may be known by his pertinent use of connections. Read any page of Johnson, you cannot alter one conjunction without spoiling the sense; it is a linked chain throughout. In your modern books, for the most part, the sentences in a page have the same connection with each other that marbles have in a bag: they touch without adhering.

THOMAS BABINGTON MACAULAY

The first rule of all writing — that rule to which every other is subordinate — is that the words used by the writer shall be such as most fully and precisely convey his meaning to the great body of his readers. All considerations about the purity and dignity of style ought to bend to this consideration. To write what is not understood in its whole force for fear of using some word which was unknown to Swift or Dryden would be, I think, as absurd as to build an observatory like that at Oxford, from which it is impossible to observe, only for the purpose of exactly preserving the proportions of the Temple of the Winds at Athens. That a word which is appropriate to a particular idea, and which expresses that idea with a completeness which is not equaled by any other single word, and scarcely by any circumlocution, should be banished from writing, seems to be a mere throwing-away of power. Such a word as 'talented' it is proper to avoid: first, because it is not wanted; secondly, because you never hear it from those who speak very good English. But the word 'shirk' as applied to military duty is a word which everybody uses; which is the word, and the only word, for the thing; which in every regiment and in every ship belonging to our country is employed ten times a day; which the Duke of Wellington, or Admiral Stopford, would use in reprimanding an officer. To interdict it, therefore, in what is meant to be familiar, and almost jocose, narrative seems to me rather rigid.

GEORGE MEREDITH

Moreover, to touch and kindle the mind through laughter demands, more than sprightliness, a most subtle delicacy. That must be a natal gift in the comic poet. The substance he deals with will show him a startling exhibition of the dyer's hand, if he is without it. People are ready to surrender themselves to witty thumps on the back, breast, and sides; all except the head — and it is there that he aims. He must be subtle to penetrate. A corresponding acuteness must exist to welcome him. The necessity for the two conditions will explain how it is that we count him during centuries in the singular number.

No one would presume to say that we are deficient in jokers. They abound, and the organization directing their machinery to shoot them in the wake of the leading article and the popular sentiment is good. But the comic differs from them in addressing the wits for laughter; and the sluggish wits want some training to respond to it, whether in public life or private, and particularly when the feelings are excited. The sense of the comic is much blunted by habits of punning and of using humoristic phrase, the trick of employing Johnsonian polysyllables to treat of the infinitely little. And it really may be humorous, of a kind; yet it will miss the point by going too much round about it.

Taking them generally, the English public are most in sympathy with this primitive Aristophanic comedy, wherein the comic is capped by the grotesque, irony tips the wit, and satire is a naked sword. They have the basis of the comic in them — an esteem for common sense. They cordially dislike the reverse of it. They have a rich laugh, though it is not the *gros rire* of the Gaul tossing *gros sel*, nor the polished Frenchman's mentally digestive laugh. And if they have now, like a monarch with a troop of dwarfs, too many jesters kicking the dictionary about, to let them *reflect* that they are dull, occasionally (like the pensive monarch surprising himself with an idea of an idea of his own), they *look* so. And they are given to looking in the glass. They must see that something ails them. How much even the better order of them will endure, without a thought of the defensive, when the person afflicting them is protected from satire, we read in memoirs of a preceding age, where the vulgarly tyrannous hostess of a great house of reception shuffled the guests and played them like a pack of cards, with her exact estimate of the strength of each one printed on them; and still this house continued to be the most popular in England, nor did the lady ever appear in print or on the boards as the comic type that she was.

You may estimate your capacity for comic perception by being able to detect the ridicule of them you love without loving them less; and more by being able to see yourself somewhat ridiculous in dear eyes, and accepting the correction their image of you proposes.

JOHN MILTON

To Charles Diodati

...What besides God has resolved concerning me I know not, but this at least: *He has instilled into me, if into any one, a vehement love of the beautiful.* Not with so much labour, as the fables have it, is Ceres said to have sought her daughter Proserpina as it is my habit day and night to seek for this *idea of the beautiful*, as for a certain image of supreme beauty, through all the forms and faces of things (*for many are the shapes of things divine*), and to follow it as it leads me on by some sure traces which I seem to recognize.

And long it was not after, when I was confirmed in this opinion, *that he who would not be frustrate of his hope to write well hereafter in laudable things ought himself to be a true poem; that is, a composition and pattern of the best and honourablest things; not presuming to sing high praises of heroic men, or famous cities, unless he have in himself the experience and the practice of all that which is praiseworthy.*

To Carlo Deodati

... I will write first. Though, if the reasons which make each of us so long in writing to the other should ever be judicially examined, it will appear that I have many more excuses for not writing than you. For it is well known, and you well know, that I am naturally slow in writing, and averse to write; while you, either from disposition or from habit, seem to have little reluctance in engaging in these literary allocutions. It is also in my favour, that your method of study is such as to admit of frequent interruptions, in which you visit your friends, write letters, or go abroad; but it is my way to suffer no impediment, no love or ease, no avocation whatever, to chill the ardour, to break the continuity, or divert the completion of my literary pursuits.

To Emeric Bigot

Thus I shall not seem to have borrowed the excellence of my literary compositions from others so much as to have drawn it pure and unmingled from the resources of my own mind and the force of my own conceptions. It gives me pleasure that you are convinced of the tranquillity which I possess under this afflicting privation of sight, as well as of the civility and kindness with which I receive those who visit me from other countries. And indeed why should I not submit with complacency to this loss of sight, which seems only withdrawn from the body without, to increase the sight of the mind within? Hence books have not incurred my resentment, nor do I intermit the study of books, though they have inflicted so heavy a penalty on me for my attachment....

FOR THE LIBERTY OF PRINTING

For, as in a body, when the blood is fresh, the spirits pure and vigorous not only to vital but to rational faculties, and those in the acutest and the pertest operations of wit and subtlety, it argues in what good plight and constitution the body is, so when the cheerfulness of the people is so sprightly up, as that it has not only wherewith to guard well its own freedom and safety, but to spare, and to bestow upon the solidest and sublimest points of controversie and new invention, it betok'ns us not degenerated, nor drooping to a fatal decay, but casting off the old and wrincl'd skin of corruption to outlive these pangs and wax young again, entring the glorious waies of Truth and prosperous vertue destin'd to become great and honourable in these latter ages. Methinks I see in my mind a noble and puissant Nation rousing herself like a strong man after sleep, and shaking her invincible locks. Methinks I see her as an Eagle muing her mighty youth, and kindling her undazzl'd eyes at the full mid-day beam, purging and unscaling her long abused sight at the fountain itself of heav'nly radiance, while the whole noise of timorous and flocking birds, with those also that love the twilight, flutter about, amaz'd at what she means, and in their envious gabble would prognosticat a year of sects and schisms.

What should ye doe then, should ye suppresse all this flowry crop of knowledge and new light, sprung up and yet springing daily in this City, should ye set an *Oligarchy* of twenty ingrossers over it, to bring a famin upon our minds again, when we shall know nothing but what is measur'd to us by their bushel? Beleeve it, Lords and Commons, they who counsell ye to such a suppressing doe as good as bid ye suppresse yourselves; and I will soon shew how. If it be desir'd to know the immediat cause of all this free writing and free speaking, there cannot be assign'd a truer then your own mild and free and human government; it is the liberty, Lords and Commons, which your own valorous and happy counsels have purchast us, liberty which is the nurse of all great wits: this is that which hath rarify'd and enlightn'd our spirits like the influence of heav'n; this is that which hath enfranchis'd, enlarg'd, and lifted up our apprehensions degrees above themselves. Ye cannot make us now lesse capable, lesse knowing, lesse eagerly pursuing of the truth, unlesse ye first make your selves, that made us so, lesse the lovers, lesse the founders of our true liberty. We can grow ignorant again, brutish, formall and slavish, as ye found us; but you then must first become that which ye cannot be, oppressive, arbitrary, and tyrannous, as they were from whom ye have free'd us. That our hearts are now more capacious, our thoughts more erected to the search and expectation of greatest and exactest things, is the issue of your owne vertu propagated in us; ye cannot suppresse that unlesse ye reinforce an abrogated and mercilesse law, that fathers may dispatch at will their own children. And who shall then sticke closest to ye, and excite others? Not he who takes up armes for cote and conduct and his four nobles of Danegelt. Although I dispraise not the defence of just immunities, yet love my peace better, if that were all. Give me the liberty to know, to utter, and to argue freely according to conscience, above all liberties.

JOHN HENRY CARDINAL NEWMAN

He writes passionately, because he feels keenly; forcibly, because he conceives vividly; he sees too clearly to be vague; he is too serious to be otiose; he can analyze his subject, and therefore he is rich; he embraces it as a whole and in its parts, and therefore he is consistent; he has a firm hold of it, and therefore he is luminous. When his imagination wells up, it overflows in ornament; when his heart is touched, it thrills along his verse. He always has the right word for the right idea, and never a word too much. If he is brief, it is because few words suffice; when he is lavish of them, still each word has its mark, and aids, not embarrasses, the vigorous march of his elocution. He expresses what all feel, but all cannot say; and his sayings pass into proverbs among his people, and his phrases become household words and idioms of their daily speech, which is tesselated with the rich fragments of his language, as we see in foreign lands the marbles of Roman grandeur worked into the walls and pavements of modern palaces.

Such pre-eminently is Shakespeare among ourselves; such pre-eminently Virgil among the Latins; such in their degree are all those writers who in every nation go by the name of Classics. To particular nations they are necessarily attached from the circumstance of the variety of tongues, and the peculiarities of each; but so far they have a catholic and ecumenical character, that what they express is common to the whole race of man, and they alone are able to express it.

WALTER PATER

An acute philosophical writer, the late Dean Mansel (a writer whose works illustrate the literary beauty there may be in closeness, and with obvious repression or economy of a fine rhetorical gift), wrote a book, of fascinating precision in a very obscure subject, to show that all the technical laws of logic are but means of securing, in each and all of its apprehensions, the unity, the strict identity with itself, of the apprehending mind. All the laws of good writing aim at a similar unity or identity of the mind in all the processes by which the word is associated to its import. The term is right, and has its essential beauty when it becomes, in a manner, what it signifies, as with the names of simple sensations. To give the phrase, the sentence, the structural member, the entire composition, song, or essay, a similar unity with its subject and with itself: — style is in the right way when it tends towards that. All depends upon the original unity, the vital wholeness and identity of the initiatory apprehension or view. So much is true of all art, which therefore requires always its logic, its comprehensive reason — insight, foresight, retrospect in simultaneous action — true, most of all, of the literary art, as being of all the arts most closely cognate to the abstract intelligence. Such logical coherency may be evidenced not merely in the lines of composition as a whole, but in the choice of a single word, while it by no means interferes with, but may even prescribe, much variety, in the building of the sentence for instance, or in the manner, argumentative, descriptive, discursive, of this or that part or member of the entire design. The blithe, crisp sentence, decisive, as a child's expression of its needs, may alternate with the long-contending, victoriously intricate sentence; the sentence born with the integrity of a single word, relieving the sort of sentence in which, if you look closely, you can see much contrivance, much adjustment, to bring a highly qualified matter into compass at one view. For the literary architecture, if it is to be rich and expressive, involves not only foresight of the end in the beginning, but also development or growth of design, in the process of execution, with many irregularities, surprises, and afterthoughts; the contingent as well as the necessary being subsumed under the unity of the whole. As truly, to the lack of such architectural design, of a single, almost visual, image, vigorously informing an entire, perhaps very intricate, composition, which shall be austere, ornate, argumentative, fanciful, yet true from first to last to that vision within, may be attributed those weaknesses of conscious or unconscious repetition of word, phrase, motive, or member of the whole matter, indicating, as Flaubert was aware, an original structure in thought not organically complete. With such foresight the actual conclusion will most often get itself written out of hand before, in the more obvious sense, the work is finished. With some strong and leading sense of the world, the tight hold of which secures true *composition* and not mere loose accretion, the literary artist, I suppose, goes on considerately, setting joint to joint, sustained by yet restraining the productive ardour, retracing the negligences of his first sketch, repeating the steps only that he may give the reader a sense of secure and restful progress, readjusting mere assonances even, that they may soothe the reader, or at least not interrupt him on his way; and then, somewhere before the end comes, is burdened, inspired, with his conclusion, and betimes delivered of it, leaving off, not in weariness and because he finds *himself* at an end, but in all the freshness of volition. His work now structurally complete, with all the accumulating effect of secondary shades of meaning, he finishes the whole up to the just proportion of that ante-penultimate conclusion, and all becomes expressive. The house he has built is rather a body he has informed. And so it happens, to its greater credit, that the better interest even of a narrative to be recounted, a story to be told, will often be in its second reading. And though there are instances of great writers who have been no artists, an unconscious tact sometimes directing work in which we may detect, very pleasurably, many of the effects of conscious art, yet one of the greatest pleasures of really good prose literature is in the critical tracing out of that conscious artistic structure, and the pervading sense of it as we read. Yes, of poetic literature, too; for, in truth, the kind of constructive intelligence here supposed is one of the forms of the imagination.

SIR WALTER RALEIGH

THE RELATION OF THE AUTHOR TO HIS AUDIENCE

At least these great artists of the sixteenth and nineteenth centuries are agreed upon one thing, that the public, even in its most gracious mood, makes an ill task-master for the man of letters. It is worth the pains to ask why, and to attempt to show how much of an author's literary quality is involved in his attitude towards his audience. Such an inquiry will take us, it is true, into bad company, and exhibit the vicious, the fatuous, and the frivolous posturing to an admiring crowd. But style is a property of all written and printed matter, so that to track it to its causes and origins is a task wherein literary criticism may profit by the humbler aid of anthropological research.

SENTIMENTALISM AND JOCULARITY

For hardier aspirants, the two main entrances to popular favour are by the twin gates of laughter and tears. Pathos knits the soul and braces the nerves, humour purges the eyesight and vivifies the sympathies; the counterfeits of these qualities work the opposite effects. It is comparatively easy to appeal to passive emotions, to play upon the melting mood of a diffuse sensibility, or to encourage the narrow mind to dispense a patron's laughter from the vantage-ground of its own small preconceptions. Our annual crop of sentimentalists and mirth-makers supplies the reading public with food. Tragedy, which brings the naked soul face to face with the austere terrors of Fate, Comedy, which turns the light inward and dissipates the mists of self-affection and self-esteem, have long since given way on the public stage to the flattery of Melodrama, under many names. In the books he reads and in the plays he sees the average man recognises himself in the hero, and vociferates his approbation.

APPROPRIATION

... There may be literary quality, it is well to remember, in the words of a parrot, if only its cage has been happily placed; meaning and soul there cannot be. Yet the voice will sometimes be mistaken, by the carelessness of chance listeners, for a genuine utterance of humanity; and the like is true in literature. But writing cannot be luminous and great save in the hands of those whose words are their own by the indefeasible title of conquest. Life is spent in learning the meaning of great words, so that some idle proverb, known for years and accepted perhaps as a truism, comes home, on a day, like a blow. 'If there were not a God,' said Voltaire, 'it would be necessary to invent him.' Voltaire had therefore a right to use the word, but some of those who use it most, if they would be perfectly sincere, should enclose it in quotation marks. Whole nations go for centuries without coining names for certain virtues; is it credible that among other peoples, where the names exist, the need for them is epidemic?

THE CONCLUSION

All style is gesture, the gesture of the mind and of the soul. Mind we have in common, inasmuch as the laws of right reason are not different for different minds. Therefore clearness and arrangement can be taught, sheer incompetence in the art of expression can be partly remedied. But who shall impose laws upon the soul? It is thus of common note that one may dislike or even hate a particular style while admiring its facility, its strength, its skilful adaptation to the matter set forth. Milton, a chaster and more unerring master of the art than Shakespeare, reveals no such lovable personality. While persons count for much, style, the index to persons, can never count for little. 'Speak,' it has been said, 'that I may know you' — voice-gesture is more than feature. Write, and after you have attained to some control over the instrument, you write yourself down whether you will or no. There is no vice, however unconscious, no virtue, however shy, no touch of meanness or of generosity in your character, that will not pass on to the paper.

JOHN RUSKIN

It seems to me, and may seem to the reader, strange that we should need to ask the question, 'What is poetry?'... I come, after some embarrassment, to the conclusion, that poetry is 'the suggestion, by the imagination, of noble grounds for the noble emotions.' I mean, by the noble emotions, those four principal secret passions — Love, Veneration, Admiration, and Joy (this latter especially, if unselfish); and their opposites — Hatred, Indignation (or Scorn), Horror, and Grief, — this last, when unselfish, becoming Compassion. These passions in their various combinations constitute what is called 'poetical feeling,' when they are felt on noble grounds, that is on great and true grounds....

Farther, it is necessary to the existence of poetry that the grounds of these feelings should be *furnished by the imagination*. Poetical feeling, that is to say, mere noble emotion, is not poetry. It is happily inherent in all human nature deserving the name, and is found often to be purest in the least sophisticated. But the power of assembling, by *the help of the imagination*, such images as will excite these feelings, is the power of the poet or literally of the 'Maker.'

Now this power of exciting the emotions depends, of course, on the richness of the imagination, and on its choice of those images which, in combination, will be most effective, or, for the particular work to be done, most fit....

The imagination has three totally distinct functions. It combines, and by combination creates new forms; but the secret principle of this combination has not been shown by the analysts. Again, it treats, or regards, both the simple images and its own combinations in peculiar ways; and thirdly, it penetrates, analyzes, and reaches truths by no other faculty discoverable....

A powerfully imaginative mind seizes and combines at the same instant, not only two, but all the important ideas of its poem or picture, and while it works with any one of them, it is at the same instant working with and modifying all in their relations to it, never losing sight of their bearings on each other; as the motion of a snake's body goes through all parts at once, and its volition acts at the same instant in coils that go contrary ways....

Every great conception of poet or painter is held and treated by this faculty (imagination). Every character that is so much as touched by men like Æschylus, Homer, Dante, or Shakespeare is by them held by the heart; and every circumstance or sentence of their being, speaking, or seeming, is seized by process from within, and is referred to that inner secret spring of which the hold is never lost for an instant; so that every sentence, as it has been thought out from the heart, opens for us a way down to the heart, leads us to the centre, and then leaves us to gather what more we may; it is the open sesame of a huge, obscure, endless cave, with inexhaustible treasure of pure gold scattered in it; the wandering about and gathering the pieces may be left to any of us, all can accomplish that, but the first opening of that invisible door in the rock is of the imagination only.

The imagination must be fed constantly by external nature.... The most imaginative men always study the hardest, and are the most thirsty for new knowledge. Fancy plays like a squirrel in its circular prison, and is happy; but imagination is a pilgrim on the earth — and her home is in heaven. Shut her from the fields of the celestial mounts — bar her from breathing their lofty, sun-warmed air; and we may as well turn upon her the last bolt of the tower of famine, and give the keys to the keeping of the wildest surge that washes Capraja and Gorgona.

SIR WALTER SCOTT

If I have a knack for anything it is for selecting the striking and interesting points out of dull details, and hence I myself receive so much pleasure and instruction from volumes which are generally reputed dull and uninteresting. Give me facts, I will find fancy for myself.

A work begun is with me a stone turned over with the purpose of rolling it down hill. The first revolutions are made with difficulty — but *vires acquirit eundo*. Now, were the said stone arrested in its progress, the whole labour would be to commence again.

Solitude's a fine thing for work, but then you must lie

by like a spider, till you collect material to continue your web.

People compliment me sometimes on the extent of my labour; but if I could employ to purpose the hours that indolence and lassitude steal away from me, they would have cause to wonder indeed. But day must have night, vigilance must have sleep, and labour, bodily or mental, must have rest.

After all, works of fiction, viz. cursed lies, are easier to write, and much more popular than the best truths.

It is clear to me that what is least forgiven in a man of any mark or likelihood is want of that article blackguardly called *pluck*. All the fine qualities of genius cannot make amends for it. We are told the genius of poets especially is irreconcilable with this species of grenadier accomplishment. If so, *quel chien de génie!*

Many people will think that because I see company easily my pleasures depend on society. But this is not the case; I am by nature a very lonely animal, and enjoy myself much at getting rid from a variety of things connected with public business, etc., which I did because they were fixed on me but I am particularly happy to be rid of.

I ought to be ashamed for having sent such Van-loads of stuff into the world, instead of which here am I *taylorizing* as my good mother would have said, that is capeing, collaring, and turning my old novels to give them novelty (?) in some degree. *Entre nous*, the success has been hitherto more than our warmest calculations anticipated. This leaves me little time for anything save exercise, which I will not give up for wealth or fame, but it cuts my correspondence sadly short.

ROBERT SOUTHEY

To Charlotte Brontë

... It is not my advice that you have asked as to the direction of your talents, but my opinion of them; and yet the opinion may be worth little, and the advice much. You evidently possess, and in no inconsiderable degree, what Wordsworth calls the 'faculty of verse.' I am not depreciating it when I say that in these times it is not rare. Many volumes of poems are now published every year without attracting public attention, any one of which, if it had appeared half a century ago, would have obtained a high reputation for its author. Whoever, therefore, is ambitious of distinction in this way ought to be prepared for disappointment.

But it is not with a view to distinction that you should cultivate this talent, if you consult your own happiness. I, who have made literature my profession, and devoted my life to it, and have never for a moment repented of the deliberate choice, think myself, nevertheless, bound in duty to caution every young man who applies as an aspirant to me for encouragement and advice against taking so perilous a course. You will say that a woman has no need of such caution; there can be no peril in it for her. In a certain sense this is true; but there is a danger of which I would, with all kindness and all earnestness, warn you. The day dreams in which you habitually indulge are likely to induce a distempered state of mind; and, in proportion as all the ordinary uses of the world seem to you flat and unprofitable, you will be unfitted for them without becoming fitted for anything else. Literature cannot be the business of a woman's life, and it ought not to be. The more she is engaged in her proper duties, the less leisure will she have for it, even as an accomplishment and a recreation. To those duties you have not yet been called, and when you are you will be less eager for celebrity. You will not seek in imagination for excitement, of which the vicissitudes of this life, and the anxieties from which you must not hope to be exempted, be your state what it may, will bring with them but too much.

But do not suppose that I disparage the gift which you possess, nor that I would discourage you from exercising it. I only exhort you so to think of it, and so to use it, as to render it conducive to your own permanent good. Write poetry for its own sake; not in a spirit of emulation, and not with a view to celebrity; the less you aim at that the more likely you will be to deserve and finally to obtain it. So written, it is wholesome both for the heart and soul; it may be made the surest means, next to religion, of soothing the mind, and elevating it. You may embody in it your best thoughts and your wisest feelings, and in so doing discipline and strengthen them.

Farewell, madam. It is not because I have forgotten that I was once young myself, that I write to you in this strain; but because I remember it. You will neither doubt my sincerity, nor my goodwill; and, however ill what has here been said may accord with your present views and temper, the longer you live the more reasonable it will appear to you. Though I may be an ungracious adviser, you will allow me, therefore, to subscribe myself, with the best wishes for your happiness here and hereafter, your true friend.

HERBERT SPENCER

We have *a priori* reasons for believing that in every sentence there is some one order of words more effective than any other; and that this order is the one which presents the elements of the proposition in the succession in which they may be most readily put together.

As in a narrative, the events should be stated in such sequence that the mind may not have to go backwards and forwards in order to rightly connect them; as in a group of sentences, the arrangement should be such, that each of them may be understood as it comes, without waiting for subsequent ones; so in every sentence, the sequence of words should be that which suggests the constituents of the thought in the order most convenient for the building up that thought.

To have a specific style is to be poor in speech. If we remember that in the far past men had only nouns and verbs to convey their ideas with, and that from then to now the growth has been towards a greater number of implements of thought, and consequently towards a greater complexity and variety in their combinations; we may infer that we are now, in our use of sentences, much what the primitive man was in his use of words; and that a continuance of the process that has hitherto gone on must produce increasing heterogeneity in our modes of expression. As now, in a fine nature, the play of the features, the tones of the voice and its cadences, vary in harmony with every thought uttered; so, in one possessed of a fully-developed power of speech, the mould in which each combination of words is cast will similarly vary with and be appropriate to the sentiment.

That a perfectly-endowed man must unconsciously write in all styles, we may infer from considering how styles originate. Why is Johnson pompous, Goldsmith simple? Why is one author abrupt, another rhythmical, another concise? Evidently in each case the habitual mode of utterance must depend upon the habitual balance of the nature. The predominant feelings have by use trained the intellect to represent them. But while long, though unconscious, discipline has made it do this efficiently, it remains, from lack of practice, incapable of doing the same for the less active feelings; and when these are excited, the usual verbal forms undergo but slight modifications. Let the powers of speech be fully developed, however — let the ability of the intellect to utter the emotions be complete; and this fixity of style will disappear. The perfect writer will express himself as Junius, when in the Junius frame of mind; when he feels as Lamb felt, will use a like familiar speech; and will fall into the ruggedness of Carlyle when in a Carlylean mood. Now he will be rhythmical and now irregular; here his language will be plain and there ornate; sometimes his sentences will be balanced and at other times unsymmetrical; for a while there will be considerable sameness, and then again great variety. His mode of expression naturally responding to his state of feeling, there will flow from his pen a composition changing to the same degree that the aspects of his subject change. He will thus without effort conform to what we have seen to be the laws of effect. And while his work presents to the reader that variety needful to prevent continuous exertion of the same faculties, it will also answer to the description of all highly-organized products, both of man and of nature: it will be, not a series of like parts simply placed in juxtaposition, but one whole made up of unlike parts that are mutually dependent.

ROBERT LOUIS STEVENSON

We have heard a story, indeed, of a painter in France who, when he wanted to paint a sea-beach, carried realism from his ends to his means, and plastered real sand upon his canvas; and that is precisely what is done in the drama. The dramatic author has to paint his beaches with real sand: real live men and women move about the stage; we hear real voices; what is feigned merely puts a sense upon what is; we do actually see a woman go behind a screen as Lady Teazle, and, after a certain interval, we do actually see her very shamefully produced again. Now all these things, that remain as they were in life, and are not transmuted into any artistic convention, are terribly stubborn and difficult to deal with; and hence there are for the dramatist many resultant limitations in time and space. These limitations in some sort approximate towards those of painting: the dramatic author is tied down, not indeed to a moment, but to the duration of each scene or act; he is confined to the stage almost as the painter is confined within his frame. But the great restriction is this, that a dramatic author must deal with his actors, and with his actors alone. Certain moments of suspense, certain significant dispositions of personages, a certain logical growth of emotion, — these are the only means at the disposal of the playwright. It is true that, with the assistance of the scene-painter, the costumier and the conductor of the orchestra, he may add to this something of pageant, something of sound and fury; but these are, for the dramatic writer, beside the mark, and do not come under the vivifying touch of his genius.

When we turn to romance, we find this no longer. Here nothing is reproduced to our senses directly. Not only the main conception of the work, but the scenery, the appliances, the mechanism by which this conception is brought home to us, have been put through the crucible of another man's mind, and come out again, one and all, in the form of written words. With the loss of every degree of such realism as we have described, there is for art a clear gain of liberty and largeness of competence. Thus painting, in which the round outlines of things are thrown on to a flat board, is far more free than sculpture, in which their solidity is preserved. It is by giving up these identities that art gains true strength. And so in the case of novels as compared with the stage. Continuous narration is the flat board on to which the novelist throws everything. And from this there results for him a great loss of vividness, but a great compensating gain in his power over the subject; so that he can now subordinate one thing to another in importance, and introduce all manner of very subtle detail, to a degree that was before impossible. He can render just as easily the flourish of trumpets before a victorious emperor and the gossip of country market women, the gradual decay of forty years of a man's life and the gesture of a passionate moment. He finds himself equally unable, if he looks at it from one point of view — equally able, if he looks at it from another point of view — to reproduce a colour, a sound, an outline, a logical argument, a physical action. He can show his readers, behind and around the personages that for the moment occupy the foreground of his story, the continual suggestion of the landscape; the turn of the weather that will turn with it men's lives and fortunes, dimly foreshadowed on the horizon; the fatality of distant events, the stream of national tendency, the salient framework of causation. And all this thrown upon the flat board — all this entering, naturally and smoothly, into the texture of continuous intelligent narration.

CHOICE OF WORDS

The art of literature stands apart from among its sisters, because the material in which their literary artist works is the dialect of life; hence, on the one hand, a strange freshness and immediacy of address to the public mind, which is ready prepared to understand it; but hence, on the other, a singular limitation. The sister arts enjoy the use of a plastic and ductile material, like the modeller's clay; literature alone is condemned to work in mosaic with finite and quite rigid words. You have seen these blocks, dear to the nursery: this one a pillar, that a pediment, a third a window or a vase. It is with blocks of just such arbitrary size and figure that the literary architect is condemned to design the palace of his art. Nor is this all; for since these blocks, or words, are the acknowledged currency of our daily affairs, there are here possible none of those suppressions by which other arts obtain relief, continuity, and vigour: no hieroglyphic touch, no smoothed impasto, no inscrutable shadow, as in painting; no blank wall, as in architecture; but every word, phrase, sentence, and paragraph must move in a logical progression, and convey a definite conventional import.

Now the first merit which attracts in the pages of a good writer, or the talk of a brilliant conversationalist, is the apt choice and contrast of the words employed. It is, indeed, a strange art to take these blocks, rudely conceived for the purpose of the market or the bar, and by tact of application touch them to the finest meanings and distinctions, restore to them their primal energy, wittily shift them to another issue, or make of them a drum to rouse the passions. But though this form of merit is without doubt the most sensible and seizing, it is far from being equally present in all writers. The effect of words in Shakespeare, their singular justice, significance, and poetic charm, is different, indeed, from the effect of words in Addison or Fielding. Or, to take an example nearer home, the words in Carlyle seem electrified into an energy of lineament, like the faces of men furiously moved; whilst the words in Macaulay, apt enough to convey his meaning, harmonious enough in sound, yet glide from the memory like undistinguished elements in a general effect. But the first class of writers have no monopoly of literary merit. There is a sense in which Addison is superior to Carlyle; a sense in which Cicero is better than Tacitus, in which Voltaire excels Montaigne: it certainly lies not in the choice of words; it lies not in the interest or value of the matter; it lies not in force of intellect, of poetry, or of humour. The three first are but infants to the three second; and yet each, in a particular point of literary art, excels his superior in the whole. What is that point?

Style is synthetic; and the artist, seeking, so to speak, a peg to plait about, takes up at once two or more elements or two or more views of the subject in hand; combines, implicates, and contrasts them; and while, in one sense, he was merely seeking an occasion for the necessary knot, he will be found, in the other, to have greatly enriched the meaning, or to have transacted the work of two sentences in the space of one. In the change from the successive shallow statements of the old chronicler to the dense and luminous flow of highly synthetic narrative, there is implied a vast amount of both philosophy and wit. The philosophy we clearly see, recognising in the synthetic writer a far more deep and stimulating view of life, and a far keener sense of the generation and affinity of events. The wit we might imagine to be lost; but it is not so, for it is just that wit, these perpetual nice contrivances, these difficulties overcome, this double purpose attained, these two oranges kept simultaneously dancing in the air, that, consciously or not, afford the reader his delight. Nay, and this wit, so little recognised, is the necessary organ of that philosophy which we so much admire. That style is therefore the most perfect, not, as fools say, which is the most natural, for the most natural is the disjointed babble of the chronicler; but which attains the highest degree of elegant and pregnant implication unobtrusively; or if obtrusively, then with the greatest gain to sense and vigour. Even the derangement of the phrases from their (so-called) natural order is luminous for the mind; and it is by the means of such designed reversal that the elements of a judgment may be most pertinently marshaled, or the stages of a complicated action most perspicuously bound into one.

There are two duties incumbent upon any man who enters on the business of writing: truth to the fact and a good spirit in the treatment. In every department of literature, though so low as hardly to deserve the name, truth to the fact is of importance to the education and comfort of mankind, and so hard to preserve, that the faithful trying to do so will lend some dignity to the man who tries it. Our judgments are based upon two things: first, upon the original preferences of our soul; but, second, upon the mass of testimony to the nature of God, man, and the universe which reaches us, in divers manners, from without. For the most part these divers manners are reducible to one, all that we learn of past times and much that we learn of our own reaching us through the medium of books or papers, and even he who cannot read learning from the same source at second-hand and by the report of him who can. Thus the sum of the contemporary knowledge or ignorance of good and evil is, in large measure, the handiwork of those who write. Those who write have to see that each man's knowledge is, as near as they can make it, answerable to the facts of life; that he shall not suppose himself an angel or a monster; nor take this world for a hell; nor be suffered to imagine that all rights are concentred in his own caste or country, or all veracities in his own parochial creed.

History is much decried; it is a tissue of errors, we are told no doubt correctly; and rival historians expose each other's blunders with gratification. Yet the worst historian has a clearer view of the period he studies than the best of us can hope to form of that in which we live. The obscurest epoch is today; and that for a thousand reasons of inchoate tendency, conflicting report, and sheer mass and multiplicity of experience; but chiefly, perhaps, by reason of an insidious shifting of landmarks. Parties and ideas continually move, but not by measurable marches on a stable course; the political soil itself steals forth by imperceptible degrees, like a travelling glacier, carrying on its bosom not only political parties but their flagposts and cantonments; so that what appears to be an eternal city founded on hills is but a flying island of Laputa.

The most influential books, and the truest in their influence, are works of fiction. They do not pin the reader to a dogma, which he must afterwards discover to be inexact; they do not teach him a lesson, which he must afterwards unlearn. They repeat, they rearrange, they clarify the lessons of life; they disengage us from ourselves, they constrain us to the acquaintance of others; and they show us the web of experience, not as we can see it for ourselves, but with a singular change — that monstrous, consuming *ego* of ours being, for the nonce, struck out. To be so, they must be reasonably true to the human comedy; and any work that is so serves the turn of instruction. But the course of our education is answered best by those poems and romances where we breathe a magnanimous atmosphere of thought and meet generous and pious characters. Shakespeare has served me best. Few living friends have had upon me an influence so strong for good as Hamlet or Rosalind.

WILLIAM MAKEPEACE THACKERAY

... The humorous writer professes to awaken and direct your love, your pity, your kindness — your scorn for untruth, pretension, imposture — your tenderness for the weak, the poor, the oppressed, the unhappy. To the best of his means and ability he comments on all the ordinary actions and passions of life. He takes upon himself to be the week-day preacher, so to speak. Accordingly, as he finds, and speaks, and feels the truth best, we regard him, esteem him — sometimes love him. And, as his business is to mark other people's lives and peculiarities, we moralize upon *his* life when he is gone — and yesterday's preacher becomes the text for to-day's sermon.

Among the sins of commission which novel-writers not seldom perpetrate, is the sin of grandiloquence, or tall talking, against which, for my part, I will offer up a special *libera me*. This is the sin of schoolmasters, governesses, critics, sermoners, and instructors of young or old people. Nay (for I am making a clean breast, and liberating my soul), perhaps of all the novel-spinners now extant the present speaker is the most addicted to preaching. Does he not stop perpetually in his story and begin to preach to you? When he ought to be engaged with business, is he not for ever taking the Muse by the sleeve, and plaguing her with some of his cynical sermons? I cry *peccavi* loudly and heartily. I tell you I would like to be able to write a story which should show no egotism whatever — in which there should be no reflections, no cynicism, no vulgarity (and so forth), but an incident in every other page, a villain, a battle, a mystery in every chapter. I should like to be able to feed a reader so spicily as to leave him hungering and thirsting for more at the end of every monthly meal.

In a pretty large experience I have not found the men who write books superior in wit or learning to those who don't write at all. In regard of mere information, non-writers must often be superior to writers. You don't expect a lawyer in full practice to be conversant with all kinds of literature; he is too busy with his law; and so a writer is commonly too busy with his own books to be able to bestow attention on the works of other people.

Have you read *David Copperfield*, by the way? How beautiful it is — how charmingly fresh and simple! In those admirable touches of tender humor — and I should call humor a mixture of love and wit — who can equal this great genius? There are little words and phrases in his books which are like personal benefits to the reader. What a place it is to hold in the affections of men! What an awful responsibility hanging over a writer! What man holding such a place, and knowing that his words go forth to vast congregations of mankind, — to grown folks — to their children, and perhaps to their children's children, — but must think of his calling with a solemn and humble heart! May love and truth guide such a man always! It is an awful prayer; may Heaven further its fulfilment!

THE CLASSICS
ARISTOTLE

It is a great matter to observe propriety in these several modes of expression — compound words, strange (or rare) words, and so forth. But the greatest thing by far is to have a command of metaphor. This alone cannot be imparted by another; it is the mark of genius — for to make good metaphors implies an eye for resemblances.

We should destroy the beauty of the most part of Homer's verses, if in the place of those choice and noble terms he used, we should put proper words. For example: When Homer says (to represent the terrible noise which the enraged sea makes): 'The rivers roar'd,' we should put, 'The rivers cried,' we should spoil it.

'Tis not the property of a poet to relate things just as they came to pass, but as they might or ought necesrarily or probably to happen. For an historian and a poet don't differ in that one writes in prose, and the other in verse; for truly Herodotus's history might very well be put into verse, and 'twould be no less a history when in verse, than 'tis now in prose. But they differ in this, that an historian writes what did happen, and a poet what might, or ought to have, come to pass.

We have laid it down that tragedy is a representation of an action that is whole and complete and of a certain magnitude, since a thing may be a whole and yet have no magnitude. A whole is what has a beginning and middle and end. A beginning is that which is not a necessary consequent of anything else but after which something else exists or happens as a natural result. An end on the contrary is that which is inevitably or, as a rule, the natural result of something else, but from which nothing else follows; a middle follows something else and something follows from it. Well constructed plots must not therefore begin and end at random, but must embody the formulæ we have stated.

Moreover, in everything that is beautiful, whether it be a living creature or any organism composed of parts, these parts must not only be well arranged but must also have a certain magnitude of their own; for beauty consists in magnitude and arrangement. From which it follows that neither would a very small creature be beautiful — for our view of it is almost instantaneous and therefore confused[1] — nor a very large one, since, being unable to view it all at once, we lose the effect of

[1] With a very small object the duration of our vision is, as it were, so rapid that the parts are invisible; we, therefore, cannot appreciate their proportion and arrangement, in which beauty consists.

a single whole; for instance, suppose a creature a thousand miles long. As then creatures and other organic structures must have a certain magnitude and yet be easily taken in by the eye, so too with plots; they must have length but must be easily taken in by the memory.

A considerable aid to clarity and distinction is the lengthening and abbreviation and alteration of words. Being otherwise than in the ordinary form and thus unusual, these will produce the effect of distinction, and clarity will be preserved by retaining part of the usual form. Those critics are therefore wrong who censure this manner of idiom and poke fun at the poet, as did the elder Eucleides,[1] who said it was easy to write poetry, granted the right to lengthen syllables at will. He had made a burlesque in this very style.

With regard to problems,[2] and the various solutions of them, how many kinds there are, and the nature of each kind, all will be clear if we look at them like this. Since the poet represents life, as a painter does or any other maker of likenesses, he must always represent one of three things — either things as they were or are; or things as they are said and seem to be; or things as they

[1] A critic of this name wrote on the drama, but his date is uncertain.

[2] A 'problem' in this sense is a difficult passage or expression which needs explanation and may easily be censured by an unsympathetic critic. Aristotle here classifies the various grounds of censure and the various lines of defence. Most of his illustrations are drawn from the critical objections lodged against the *Iliad* and by Zoilus and other 'hammerers of Homer.' As the reader will see, many of them are abysmally foolish.

should be. These are expressed in diction with or without rare words and metaphors, there being many modifications of diction, all of which we allow the poet to use. Moreover, the standard of what is correct is not the same in the art of poetry as it is in the art of life or any other art. In the actual art of poetry there are two kinds of errors, essential and accidental. If a man meant to represent something and failed through incapacity, that is an essential error. But if his error is due to his original conception being wrong and his portraying, for example, a horse advancing both its right legs, that is then a technical error in some special branch of knowledge, in medicine, say, or whatever it may be; or else some sort of impossibility has been portrayed, but that is not an essential error. These considerations must, then, be kept in view in meeting the charges contained in these objections.

Let us first take the charges against the art of poetry itself. If an impossibility has been portrayed, an error has been made. But it is all right if the poet thus achieves the object of poetry — what that is has been already stated — and makes that part or some other part of the poem more striking. The pursuit of Hector is an example of this.[1] If, however, the object could have been achieved better or just as well without sacrifice of technical accuracy, then he has not done well, for, if possible there should be no error at all in any part

---

[1] *Iliad*, XXII, 205 *sq*. 'And to the host divine Achilles nodded with his head a sign and let them not launch their bitter darts at Hector, lest another should win glory by shooting him and Achilles himself come second.'

of the poem. Again, one must ask of which kind is the error, is it an error in poetic art or a chance error in some other field? It is less of an error not to know that a female stag has no horns than to make a picture that is unrecognizable.

DEMETRIUS

The best literary style is that which is pleasant to read; and this is the style which is compacted and (as it were) consolidated by the conjunctions.

Words should be marshaled in the following way. First should be placed those that are not especially vivid; in the second or last place should come those that are distinctly so. In this way what comes first will strike the ear as vivid, and what follows as more vivid still. Failing this, we shall seem to have lost vigor, and (so to speak) to have lapsed from strength to weakness.

An illustration will be found in a passage of Plato: 'when a man suffers music to play upon him and to flood his soul through his ears.' (*a*) Here the second expression is far more vivid than the first. And farther on he says: 'but when he ceases not to flood it, nay throws a spell over it, thereupon he causes it to melt and waste away.' (*b*) The word 'waste' is more striking than the word 'melt,' and approaches more nearly to poetry. If Plato had reversed the order, the verb 'melt,' coming later, would have appeared too weak.

DIONYSIUS

...Genius, it is said, is born and does not come of teaching, and the only art for producing it is nature. Works of natural genius, so people think, are spoiled and utterly demeaned by being reduced to the dry bones of rule and precept. For my part I hold that the opposite may be proved, if we consider that, while in lofty emotion Nature for the most part knows no law, yet it is not the way of Nature to work at random and wholly without system. In all production Nature is the prime cause, the great exemplar; but as to all questions of degree, of the happy moment in each case, and again of the safest rules of practice and use, such prescriptions are the proper contribution of an art or system. We must remember also that mere grandeur runs the greater risk, if left to itself without the stay and ballast of scientific method, and abandoned to the impetus of uninstructed enterprise. For genius needs the curb as often as the spur. Speaking of the common life of men, Demosthenes [1] declares that the greatest of all blessings is good fortune, and that next comes good judgment, which is indeed quite as important, since the lack of it often completely cancels the advantage of the former.

[1] *Aristocrates*, 113.

We may apply this to literature and say that Nature fills the place of good fortune, Art that of good judgment. And above all we must remember this: the very fact that in literature some effects come of natural genius alone can only be learnth from art.

There are, one may say, some five genuine sources of the sublime in literature, the common groundwork, as it were, of all five being a natural faculty of expression, without which nothing can be done. The first and most powerful is the command of full-blooded ideas [1] — I have defined this in my book on Xenophon — and the second is the inspiration of vehement emotion. These two constituents of the sublime are for the most part congenital. But the other three come partly of art, namely the proper construction of figures — these being probably of two kinds, figures of thought and figures of speech — and, over and above these, nobility of phrase, which again may be resolved into choice of words and the use of metaphor and poetic ornament. The fifth cause of grandeur, which embraces all those already mentioned, is the general effect of dignity and elevation.[2]

[1] ἁδρός means 'solid,' 'robust,' and is used in literary criticism in a sense similar to δεινός, 'vehement.' 'Weighty and solid thought' is the meaning. The book on Xenophon is lost; perhaps he means merely 'remarks on Xenophon' in some other treatise.

[2] The five 'sources' are: (1) the command of full-blooded ideas; (2) emotion; (3) the proper use of 'figures'; (4) nobility of phrase; (5) general effect. Elsewhere σύνθεσις means the arrangement of words. Here the phrase seems to mean the putting together of the words and clauses into a total effect of grandeur, making a *whole* of them.

Weight, grandeur, and energy in writing are very largely produced, dear pupil, by the use of 'images.' (That at least is what some people call the actual mental pictures.) For the term imagination is applied in general to an idea which enters the mind from any source and engenders speech, but the word has now come to be used of passages where, inspired by strong emotion, you seem to see what you describe and bring it vividly before the eyes of your audience. That imagination means one thing in oratory and another in poetry you will yourself detect, and also that the object of poetry is to enthral,[1] of prose writing to present ideas clearly, though both indeed aim at this latter and at excited feeling.

HORACE

First, be it understood, I make no claim
To rank with those who bear a poet's name:
'Tis not enough to turn out lines complete,
Each with its proper quantum of five feet;
Colloquial verse a man may write like me,
But (trust an author) 'tis not poetry.
No; keep that name for genius, for a soul
Of Heaven's own fire, for words that grandly roll.
Hence some have questioned if the Muse we call
The Comic Muse be really one at all:

[1] ἔκπληξις means startling people out of their wits, emotional illusion.

Her subject ne'er aspires, her style ne'er glows,
And, save that she talks metre, she talks prose.
'Ay but the angry father shakes the stage,
When on his graceless son he pours his rage.'...
Well, could Pomponius' sire to life return,
Think you he'd rate his son in tones less stern?
So then 'tis not sufficient to combine
Well-chosen words in a well-ordered line,
When, take away the rhythm, the self-same words
Would suit an angry father off the boards.
Strip what I write, or what Lucilius wrote,
Of cadence and succession, time and note,
Reverse the order, put those words behind
That went before, no poetry you'll find:
But break up this, 'When battle's brazen door
Blood-boltered Discord from its fastenings tore,'
'Tis Orpheus mangled by the Mænads: still
The bard remains, unlimb him as you will.
My friends, make Greece your model when you write,
And turn her volumes over day and night.
'But Plautus pleased our sires, the good old folks:
They praised his numbers and they praised his jokes.'
They did: 'twas mighty tolerant in them
To praise, where wisdom would perhaps condemn;
That is, if you and I and our compeers
Can trust our tastes, our fingers, and our ears,
Know polished wit from horse-play, and can tell
What verses do, and who do not run well.

(After a brief sketch of the progress of Tragedy and Comedy in Greece, he continues):

Our poets have tried all things; nor do they
Deserve least praise, who follow their own way,
And tell in comedy or history-piece
Some story of home-growth, not drawn from Greece.
Nor would the land we love be now more strong
In warrior's prowess than in poet's song,
Did not her bards with one consent decline
The tedious task, to alter and refine.
Dear Pisos! as you prize old Numa's blood,
Set down that work, and that alone, as good,
Which, blurred and blotted, checked and counter-checked,
Has stood all tests, and issued forth correct.
Because Democritus thinks fit to say,
That wretched art to genius must give way,[1]
Stands at the gate of Helicon, and guards
Its precinct against all but crazy bards,
But here occurs a question some men start,
If good verse comes from nature or from art.
For me, I cannot see how native wit
Can e'er dispense with art, or art with it.
Set them to pull together, they're agreed,
And each supplies what each is found to need.

[1] It is only fair to Horace to add his views on the relation of art and 'inspiration' which occur later in the treatise.

In words again be cautious and select,
And duly pick out this, and that reject.
High praise and honor to the bard is due
Whose dexterous setting makes an old word new.
Nay more, should some recondite subject need
Fresh signs to make it clear to those who read,
A power of issuing terms till now unused,
If claimed with modesty, is ne'er refused.
New words will find acceptance, if they flow
Forth from the Greek, with just a twist or so.
But why should Rome capriciously forbid
Our bards from doing what their fathers did?
Or why should Plautus and Cæcilius gain
What Virgil or what Varius asks in vain?
Nay, I myself, if with my scanty wit
I coin a word or two, why grudge me it,
When Ennius and old Cato boldly flung
Their terms broadcast, and amplified our tongue?
To utter words stamped current by the mill
Has always been thought right and always will.
   When forests shed their foliage at the fall,
The earliest born still drops the first of all:
So fades the elder race of words, and so
The younger generations bloom and grow.

(Of the lines next quoted a competent critic (W. Y. Sellar, 'Horace and the Elegiac Poets,' p. 110) says that they 'are not only as admirable practical advice on the cultivation of style as any ever given, but explain the secret of Horace's own ease in writing.' Even those who censure Horace for his 'golden mediocrity' and his want of deep feeling admit the essential charm and beauty which invest his picture of the ideal Latin poet.)

> Bad poets are our jest; yet they delight,
> Just like their betters, in whate'er they write,
> Hug their fool's paradise, and, if you're slack
> To give them praise, themselves supply the lack.
> But he who meditates a work of art,
> Oft as he writes, will act the censor's part:
> Is there a word wants nobleness and grace,
> Devoid of weight, unworthy of high place?
> He bids it go, though stiffly it decline,
> And cling and cling, like suppliant to a shrine:
> Choice terms, long hidden from the general view,
> He brings to day and dignifies anew,
> Which, once on Cato's and Cethegus' lips,
> Now pale their light and suffer dim eclipse;
> New phrases, in the world of books unknown,
> So use but father them, he makes his own:
> Fluent and limpid, like a crystal stream,
> He makes Rome's soil with genial produce teem.

PLATO

Is not the power of appearance that deceiving art which makes us wander up and down and take the things at one time of which we repent at another, both in our actions and in our choice of things great and small? But the art of measurement is that which would do away with the effect of appearances, and, showing the truth, would fain teach the soul at last to find rest in the truth, and would thus save our life.

FRENCH WRITERS
HONORÉ DE BALZAC

I have resumed my life of toil. I go to bed at six, directly after dinner. The animal digests and sleeps till midnight. Auguste makes me a cup of coffee, with which the mind goes at one flash (*tout d'une traite*) till midday. I rush to the printing-office to carry my copy and get my proofs, which gives exercise to the animal, who dreams as he goes.

One can put a good deal of black on white in twelve hours, little sister, and after a month of such life there's no small work accomplished. Poor pen! it must be made of diamond not to be worn out by such toil! To lift its master to reputation, according to the prophecy of the Germans, to pay his debts to all, and then to give him, some day, rest upon a mountain — that is its task!

But if you knew me personally, if my solitary life, my days of study, privation, and toil were told to you, you would lay aside some of your accusations and perceive more than one antithesis between the man and his writings. Certainly there are some works in which I like to be myself; but you can guess them; they are those in which the heart speaks out. My fate is to paint the happiness that others feel; to desire it in perfection, but never to meet it. None but those who suffer can paint joy, because we express better that which we conceive than that we have experienced.

I work eighteen hours a day. I have perceived the faults of style which disfigure *La Peau de Chagrin*. I corrected them to make it irreproachable; but after two months' labor, the volume being reprinted, I discover another hundred faults. Such are the sorrows of a poet.

But I need time for all these conceptions, and especially for their execution; above all when (as for *Séraphita*) I work often a year or two in thought before taking a pen. *Adoremus in aeternum* means for me, 'Toil ever.'

It is true that I go out little and sit at my work for twenty hours.

My letters are becoming short, you say, and you no longer know whom I see. I see no one; I work so continually that I have not a moment for writing. But I do have moments of lassitude for thinking. Some day you will be astonished at what I have been able to do, and yet write to a friend at all.

Listen: to settle this point, reflect on this: Walter Scott wrote two novels a year, and was thought to have luck in his labour; he astonished England. This year I shall have produced: (1) *Le Père Goriot;* (2) *Le Lys dans la Vallée;* (3) *Les Mémoires d'une jeune Mariée;* (4) *César Birotteau*. I have done three parts of the *Etudes de Mœurs* for Madame Bêchet; and three parts of the *Etudes Philosophiques* for Werdet. And finally, I shall have finished the third *dizain*, and *Séraphita*. But then, shall I be living, or in my sound mind in 1836? I doubt it. Sometimes I think that my brain is inflaming. I shall die on the breach of intellect.

You understand that in a literary campaign like mine society is impossible. Therefore I have openly renounced it. I go nowhere, I answer no letter and no invitation. I only allow myself the Italian opera *once* a fortnight.

Like the fisherman in Walter Scott's *Antiquary*, I must saw my plank without risking the blunder of an inch; I must write. Oh! *cara*, write! when one's soul is mourning, and when the sister-soul is mourning also, and something is lost to us of our faith in losing the soul that inspired it! — Let us bury that secret in our hearts.

If you only knew how, after this solitary life, I long to grasp Nature by a rapid rush across Europe, how my soul thirsts for the immense, the infinite; for Nature seen in the mass, not in detail, judged on its grand lines, sometimes damp with rain, sometimes rich with sun, as we bound across space, seeing lands instead of villages. If you knew this you would not tell me to come, for that redoubles my torture, it fans the furnace on which I sleep.

As you say, one must try to penetrate the meaning of *Séraphita* in order to criticise the work; but I never counted on a success after *Louis Lambert* was so despised. These are books that I make for myself and a few others. When I have to write a book for all the world I know very well what ideas to appeal to, and what I must express. *Séraphita* has nothing of earth; if she loved, if she doubted, if she suffered, if she were influenceable by anything terrestrial, she would not be the angel.

When a book is done, I like to forget it; I do forget it; and I never return to it except to purge it of its faults a year or two later.

FRANÇOIS RENÉ VICOMTE DE CHATEAUBRIAND

I have explored the seas of the Old World and the New, and trod the soil of the four quarters of the globe. After camping in Iroquois shelters and Arab tents, in the wigwams of the Hurons, amid the remains of Athens, Jerusalem, Memphis, Carthage, Grenada, among Greeks, Turks and Moors, in forests and among ruins; after wearing the bearskin of the savage and the silken caftan of the mameluke; after enduring poverty, hunger, thirst, and exile, I have sat, as minister and ambassador, in a gold-laced coat, my breast motley with stars and ribbons, at the tables of kings, at the feasts of princes and princesses, only to relapse into indigence and to receive a taste of prison....

I have endless materials in my possession; more than four thousand private letters, the diplomatic correspondence of my several embassies, that of my term at the Foreign Office, including documents of a unique character, known to none save myself. I have carried the soldier's musket, the traveler's cudgel, the pilgrim's staff: I have been a sea-farer, and my destinies have been as fickle as my sails; a halcyon, and made my nest upon the billows.

When death lowers the curtain between me and the

world, it shall be found that my drama was divided into three acts.

From my early youth until 1800, I was a soldier and a traveler; from 1800 to 1811, under the Consulate and the Empire, my life was given to literature; from the Restoration to the present day, it has been devoted to politics.

Of the modern French authors of my own period, I may be said to be the only one whose life resembles his works; a traveler, soldier, poet, publicist, it is amid forest that I have sung the forest, aboard ship that I have depicted the sea, in camp that I have spoken of arms, in exile that I have learnt to know exile, in Courts, in affairs of State, in Parliament that I have studied princes, politics, law, and history.

Reading aloud to others my first rough drafts helped to enlighten me. Reading aloud is an excellent form of instruction, when one does not take the necessary compliments for gospel. Provided an author be in earnest, he will soon feel, through the impression which he instinctively receives from the others, which are the weak places in his work, and especially whether that work is too long or too short, whether he keeps, does not reach, or exceeds the right dimensions.

VICOMTE DE CHATEAUBRIAND 183

Shakespeare is of the number of the five or six writers who have sufficed for the needs and nutriment of thought: those parent geniuses seem to have brought forth and suckled all the others. Homer impregnated antiquity: Æschylus, Sophocles, Euripides, Aristophanes, Horace, Virgil are his sons. Dante engendered Modern Italy, from Petrarch to Tasso. Rabelais created French literature: Montaigne, La Fontaine, Molière descend from him. England is all Shakespeare, and in these later days he has lent his language to Byron, his dialogue to Walter Scott.

Men often disown these supreme masters; they rebel against them;... but they struggle in vain against their yoke.... They open out horizons whence burst forth sheaves of light; they sow ideas, the germs of a thousand others; they supply all the arts with imaginations, subjects, styles: their works are the mines or the bowels of the human mind.

These geniuses occupy the first rank; their vastness, their variety, their fruitfulness, their originality cause them to be accepted from the very first as laws, models, moulds, types of the various forms of intellect, even as there are four or five races of men issuing from one single stock, of which the others are only branches.

None is a competent judge, in living literature, of other than works written in his own tongue. It is in vain that you believe yourself thoroughly acquainted with a foreign idiom:... certain accents belong to the mother country alone.

In short, for the sake of our own glory and for that of our works, we cannot too much attach ourselves to virtue; it is the beauty of the sentiments which creates beauty of style. When the soul is elevated the words fall from on high, and nobleness of expression will always follow nobleness of thought. Horace and the Stagyrite do not teach the whole of the art: there are delicacies and mysteries of language which can only be communicated to the writer by the probity of his own heart, and which can never be taught by the precepts of rhetoric.

DENIS DIDEROT

A EULOGY OF RICHARDSON

(The author of *Pamela*, *Clarissa*, and *Sir Charles Grandison*.)

Until the present day a novel was considered a frivolous tissue of fanciful events, the study of which was dangerous to our tastes and our morals. I much wish that some other name could be given to Richardson's works, which, indeed, are styled novels, yet which elevate the mind, touch our nobler feelings, and breathe throughout a love of goodness.

The maxims which Montaigne, Charron, La Rochefoucauld, and Nicole wrote down are given by Richardson in a living form in his characters. A clever man may be able to reproduce the maxims of the moralists, but these maxims will not enable him to re-write or correct a page of Richardson.[1]

A maxim is a general and abstract rule of conduct, the application of which is left to ourselves. By itself it offers no striking picture to our minds; but when we watch a man's actions, then we put ourselves in his place, or by his side, and we take part for or against him. If he is virtuous we sympathize with him, and if he is unjust or vicious we turn from him with indignation. Who has not shuddered at the character of Lovelace and Tomlinson? Who has not been filled with horror to see such a wretch feigning all the virtues with such an air of candor and dignity, with such a semblance of pathos and truth? What reader has not confessed in his inmost heart that he would be forced to fly society and to seek the solitude of the woods if there were many such dissemblers as these? Yes, Richardson, in spite of ourselves you compel us to take our part on your stage, to join in the conversations, to approve, to blame, to admire, to be angry or indignant.

[1] The Emperor Napoleon, when writing to M. Bardier from Bayonne in 1808 about a traveling library, expressed a wish that, out of 1000 volumes, 100 should be novels, and added: 'The novels should, of course, comprise, in addition to the Nouvelle Héloise, Rousseau's Confessions, and some of Voltaire's stories, the best works of Fielding, Richardson, and Le Sage.' [Translator's note.]

If it is important that men should be impressed with the fact that, without regard to any future state, the best way to be happy is to be virtuous, what a great service Richardson has done to mankind! He has not proved this truth, but he has made us feel it. In every line he writes he makes us choose by preference the side of oppressed virtue rather than that of triumphant vice.

Who would wish to be Lovelace in spite of all his advantages? Who would not prefer to be Clarissa in spite of all her misfortunes?

I cannot weary of admiring your capacious intellect, which could carry on a drama of thirty or forty persons, who all act according to the characters you have given them. You show an astonishing knowledge of the laws and customs and manners of the human heart and of life. How much you must have observed, and felt, and weighed in the moral balance.

Poets, learn from Richardson to give an accomplice to the villain of your piece, in order to lessen the horror of his crime, and, for just the opposite reason, do not give a companion to your virtuous hero, that he may stand alone in his merit.

One poet said of another poet: *He will not go far, he*

has not found the secret. What secret? That of describing objects of real interest, fathers, mothers, husbands, wives, children.

O, my friend, how long and difficult and painful is the study of all these arts, whether painting or sculpture, music or poetry, carving or engraving, where we seek to imitate nature.

I think I have already remarked in some of my papers (where I meant to show that a nation could only have one grand century, and that in this grand century there was only one moment able to give birth to a great man) that every fine composition, and every real work of talent in painting, sculpture, architecture, eloquence, and poetry, presupposes a certain mingling of reason and enthusiasm, of judgment and impulse, in the artist's disposition: a disposition which is rarely found, and only rarely manifested — an equilibrium of qualities without which an artist's productions are cold or extravagant.

ALEXANDRE DUMAS (PÈRE)

Comparatively speaking, the making of *Henri III* was speedy: when the plot was once clearly set out in my mind, I took barely two months to complete the work.

I remember that in the interval between the shaping of the plot and the writing of the play, I went down to Villers-Cotterets — for the shooting, I think. On my way back I walked on in front of the coach, and my young friends Saunier, Labarre, and Duez accompanied me as far as the village of Vauciennes. On the road I recited *Henri III* to them, from beginning to end: *Henri III* was made directly its plot was made.

And, in fact, whenever I am engaged upon a work which occupies all my thoughts, I feel the need of narrating it aloud; in narrating, I invent; and at the end of one or other of these recitals, I find some fine morning that the play is completed. But it often happens that this method of working — that is to say, not beginning the piece until I have finished the plot — is a very slow one. In this way I kept *Mademoiselle de Belleisle* for nearly five years in my head; and ever since 1832 I have had in my mind the outline of a *Juif Errant*, to which I can devote myself at the first leisure moment I get, and which will be one of my best books. Indeed, I have only one fear, which is that I may die without having written it.

When *Henri III* was completed, I read it at Madame Waldor's before an informal committee. The play produced a great effect, but the unanimous opinion was that I ought to get *Christine* produced before it: *Henri III*, they said, was too hazardous for a first venture. I need not say that dear old M. Villenave looked upon all these new attempts as monstrous, and pronounced them to be aberrations of the human intellect.

I had made the acquaintance of a young doctor, by name Thibaut.

Thibaut knew exactly all these things that I did not know, and he undertook the rough task of my education. We passed most of our evenings together in a little room in the Rue du Pélican, looking out over the Véro-Dodat passage. I was only a hundred yards from the Palais-Royal, so could easily slip round there to make up the letter-bag.

In the mornings I sometimes accompanied Thibaut to the Charité hospital, and did a little physiology and anatomy — though I could never overcome my repugnance to operations and corpses. From these visits came a certain amount of medical or surgical knowledge, which has more than once been of use to me in my novels.

Thus, for example, in *Amaury*, in the case of Madeleine my heroine, I traced the phases of a lung disease....

In another direction, following the advice of Lassagne, I set myself to reading, and I began with Walter Scott. The first novel I read, signed by the 'Scotch

Bard' — so the phrase went at that time — was *Ivanhoe*.

Then came Cooper, with his mighty forests, immense prairies, and boundless oceans — his *Pioneers*, his *Prairie*, his *Red Rover* — three masterpieces of description, in which the lack of substance is so well veiled by richness of form that you go right through the romance, treading, like the apostle, on ground always ready to open and engulf you, and yet you are upheld, not by faith, but by poetry, from the first page even to the last.

And then Byron — Byron who died at Missolonghi, just when I was beginning to study at Paris as a dramatic and lyric poet.

The speculation was not a fortunate one for either of us, and so I laid to heart a piece of advice given me by a shrewd publisher, one M. Bossange:

'Make yourself a name, and I will print you.'

Ay, there was the whole question, *Make yourself a name!* That is the condition at one time set before every man who has made himself a name — the condition of which, at the moment when it was imposed on him, he asked himself in despair, 'How can I fulfill it?' And yet he has fulfilled it. For my part, I am no believer in talent ignored or genius misunderstood.

So I set to work in earnest to make my name, in order that I might sell my books and have no more of the half-profit system. And indeed this name, small and modest as it was, was beginning to show through the ground....

So I counted for something in contemporary literature, since Vatout asked me for verses.

I had seen *Hamlet, Romeo, Shylock, Othello, Richard III, Macbeth.* I had read — nay, devoured — not only the repertory of Shakspeare, but that of every foreign dramatic poet; and I had come to recognise that in the world of the theatre everything emanates from Shakespeare, as in the real world all emanates from the sun — Shakespeare, to whom none other can be compared, and who, coming before all the others, still remains as tragical as Corneille, as comical as Molière, as original as Calderon, as philosophic as Goethe, as impassioned as Schiller. I recognised that the works of this one man contained as many types as those of all the rest put together. I recognised, in fine, that he was the one who had created most — next after God....

But, at the same time, I was under no delusion about the difficulties of the career to which I was devoting my life. I knew that, more than any other, it was a career which demanded special and profound study, and that, if you are to experiment with success upon living nature, you must first have long and carefully studied dead nature. I did not, therefore, content myself with a preliminary survey. I took, one after the other, those men of genius whose names are Shakespeare, Molière,

Corneille, Calderon, Goethe, Schiller. I spread out their works, like corpses on the table of a dissecting room, and, scalpel in hand, whole nights through, I penetrated to the very heart to discover the sources of life and the secret of the blood's circulation. And at last I gained an insight into that admirable mechanism which could set nerves and muscles in play — that skill which could model teguments of flesh so various, and yet designed to cover bones essentially the same. For man does not invent. God has handed creation over to him, and it is for him to apply it to his needs. Progress is but the conquest — through days, through months, through generations — the conquest of matter by man. Each one of us comes in his turn and in his hour, enters upon the inheritance of the things discovered by his fathers, sets these to work by fresh combinations, then dies, after having added to the sum of human knowledge, which he bequeaths to his sons, some new fragment — one star in the Milky Way!

And so it was not merely my special dramatic work, but my dramatic education, that I was bringing to a completion. Nay, I am wrong; the work is finished some day, the education never.

GUSTAVE FLAUBERT

I even think that a novelist *has not the right to express his own opinion* on any subject whatever. He may communicate it, but I do not like him to say it. (That is part of my art of poetry.) I limit myself, then, to declaring things as they appear to me, to expressing what seems to be true, and the devil take the consequences; rich or poor, victors or vanquished, I admit none of all that. I want neither love nor hate, nor pity nor anger. Great art is scientific and impersonal.

When you take up a book you must swallow it at one mouthful. That is the only way to know it in its entirety. Accustom yourself to follow out an idea.

I am but a lizard, a literary lizard, warming himself all day long at the full sun of the beautiful.

As for me, the more I feel the difficulties of good writing, the more my boldness grows. It is this preserves me from the pedantry into which I should otherwise fall. I have plans for books, the composition of which would occupy the rest of my life; and if there happen to me, sometimes, cruel moments, which wellnigh make me weep with anger (so great do I feel my weakness to be), there are others also when I can scarce contain myself for joy: something from the depth within me, for which voluptuous is no word, overflows for me in sudden leaps. I feel transported, almost inebriate, with my own thoughts, as if there came to me, at some window within, a puff of warm perfumes. I shall never go very far, and know how much I lack; but the task I undertake will surely be executed by another. I shall have put on the true road some one better endowed, better born, for the purpose, than myself. The determination to give to prose the rhythm of verse, leaving it still veritable prose; to write the story of common life as history or the epic gets written (that is to say, without detriment to the natural truth of the subject) is perhaps impossible. I ask myself the question sometimes. Yet it is perhaps a considerable, an original thing, to have tried. I shall have had my permanent value for my obstinacy. And who knows? One day I may find a good *motif*, and air entirely within the compass of my voice; and at any rate I shall have passed my life not ignobly, often with delight. Yet still it is saddening to think how many great men arrive easily at the desired effect, by means beyond the limits of conscious art. What could be worse built than many things in Rabelais, Cervantes, Molière, Hugo? But, then, what sudden thrusts of power! What power in a single word!

Style, as I conceive it, style as it will be realised some day — in ten years, or ten generations! It would be rhythmical as verse itself, precise as the language of science; and with undulations — a swelling of the violin! plumage of fire! A style which would enter into the idea like the point of a lancet; when thought would travel over the smooth surfaces like a canoe with fair winds behind it. Prose is but of yesterday, it must be confessed. Verse is *par excellence* the form of the ancient literatures. All possible prosodic combinations have been already made; those of prose are still to make.

The cause of my going so slowly is just this, that nothing in that book (*Madame Bovary*) is drawn from myself. Never has my personality been so useless to me. It may be, perhaps, that hereafter I shall do stronger things. I hope so, but I can hardly imagine I shall do anything more skilful. Here everything is of the head. If it has been false in aim, I shall always feel that it has been a good mental exercise. But after all, what is the non-natural to others is the natural to me — the extraordinary, the fantastic, the wild chase, mythologic, or metaphysic. *Saint Antoine* did not require of me one quarter of the tension of mind *Madame Bovary* has caused me. *Saint Antoine* was a discharge; I had nothing but pleasure in writing it; and the eighteen months devoted to the composition of its five hundred pages were the most thoroughly voluptuous of my life, hitherto. Judge then of my condition in writing *Madame Bovary*. I must needs put myself every minute into a skin not mine, and antipathetic to me. For six months now I have been making love Platonically; and at the present moment my exaltation of mind is that of a good Catholic: I am longing to go to confession.

Posterity will not be slow in cruel desertion of those who have determined to be useful, and have sung for a cause. It cares very little for Chateaubriand, and his resuscitation of mediæval religion; for Béranger, with his libertine philosophy; will soon care little for Lamartine and his religious humanitarianism. Truth is never in the present; and if one attaches oneself to the present, there comes an end of one. At the present moment, I believe that even a thinker (and the artist, surely, is three times a thinker) should have no convictions.

There is no imagination in France. If you want to make real poetry pass, you must be clever enough to disguise it.

In youth one associates the future realization of one's dreams with the existence of the actual people around us. In proportion as those existences disappear, our dreams also depart.

Nothing is more useless than those heroic friendships which require exceptional circumstances to prove them. The great difficulty is to find some one who does not rack your nerves in every one of the various ordinary occurrences of life.

Formerly, people believed that the sugar-cane alone yielded sugar; nowadays it is extracted from almost anything. It is the same with poetry. Let us draw it, no matter whence, for it lies everywhere, and in all things. Let us habituate ourselves to regard the world as a work of art, the processes of which are to be reproduced in our works.

Fresh proofs, fresh corrections. This time is the turn for 'weeding.' The dog-grass that has sprung up must be torn out; the 'which's,' 'who's,' and 'whose's,' and 'whereof's.' They give the best style a crick in the neck. Banish too the semicolon, that bastard stop that is neither full stop nor comma. It was perfect for the days of complimentary speeches, long discourses, and funeral orations. It gave repose to the flowing period. But we live in the day of the pneumatic and the telephone. Whenever you can shorten a sentence, do. And one always can. The best sentence? The shortest.

Beware of finely spacious and melodious phrases. First they gently rock you, then send you to sleep. As for transitions, don't give a fig for them. The best way of concealing from the reader your passage from one thing to another is to take it in a quick jump, without boggling.

Verbal repetitions? In a writer worthy of the name —

remember this — there are no such things. Doubtless, after the first rush, you will find in my paragraphs a word that comes over and over again. That is the *leit-motif* of the symphony. Be careful not to delete and replace it by a synonym. Real synonyms do not exist. Why should I stultify myself? When I used the word that you shy at, I had imperative reasons for it. If it seems tedious when it turns up again, that is only because it is badly placed. Respect the word. Cut up the sentence. Bring the scissors into play. The scissors! Ah, who could rightly celebrate their usefulness to literature? The perfect writer is always represented with a goose-quill between his fingers. That is his weapon, his heraldic arms. Now I should like to be painted wielding my scissors, like a dressmaker.

ANATOLE FRANCE

I thank fate for having made me be born poor. Poverty taught me the true value of the gifts useful to life.

... there is no objective criticism. The good critic is the one who relates the adventures of his soul in the midst of masterpieces.

I have always been inclined to take life as a spectacle.

I am sure of very few things in this world.... I should be tempted to put very large question-marks after all that I write, all that I say, and all that I think.

The rights of thought are superior to all.... Let us not distrust thought. Far from subjecting it to our morality, let us subject to it everything else. Thought is all of man. We know only one reality, thought. It is thought that creates the universe.

Suffering! we owe to it all that is good in us, all that gives value to life; we owe to it pity, we owe to it courage, we owe to it all the virtues.

I know that composition usually passes for the first necessity of the art of writing. One recognizes in their (Rabelais and Cervantes) works a far sturdier unity than that of a skilfully woven plot. It is the coherence of their mind. The best books, in my opinion, he says, are those that give the most food for thought, and on the most diverse things.

The only thing that counts, style.
The finest words in the world are only vain sounds, if you cannot comprehend them.

Words are ideas. One reasons correctly only with strict syntax and a precise vocabulary.

Born writers make their own rule, or rather, they have none. They change style at every moment, at the dictation of inspiration.

If there is no really simple style, there are styles that appear simple, and precisely these seem destined to eternal youth. They owe this fortunate appearance not to the fact that they are less rich than the others in diverse elements, but to the fact that they form a whole in which all the parts are so well blended as to be indistinguishable.... Simple style is like white light. It is complex but its complexity is not obvious.

Every thinker in the world has said it or will say it: Ernest Renan was, of all our contemporaries, the one who exercised the greatest influence on cultivated minds and who added the most to their culture.

VICTOR HUGO

Great men rarely come alone; large trees seem larger when they dominate a forest; there they are at home. There was a forest of minds around Voltaire; that forest was the eighteenth century. Among those minds there were summits, Montesquieu, Buffon, Beaumarchais, and among others, two, the highest after Voltaire — Rousseau and Diderot.

Those thinkers taught men to reason; reasoning well

leads to acting well; justness in the mind becomes justice in the heart. Those toilers for progress labored usefully. Buffon founded naturalism; Beaumarchais discovered, outside of Molière, a kind of comedy till then unknown, almost the social comedy; Montesquieu made in law some excavations so profound that he succeeded in exhuming the right. As to Rousseau, as to Diderot, let us pronounce those two names apart; Diderot, a vast intelligence, inquisitive, a tender heart, a thirst for justice, wished to give certain notions as the foundation of true ideas, and created the Encyclopædia. Rousseau rendered to woman an admirable service, completing the mother by the nurse, placing near one another those two majesties of the cradle. Rousseau, a writer, eloquent and pathetic, a profound oratorical dreamer, often divined and proclaimed political truth; his ideal borders upon the real; he had the glory of being the first man in France who called himself citizen. The civic fibre vibrates in Rousseau; that which vibrates in Voltaire is the universal fibre. One can say that in the fruitful eighteenth century Rousseau represented the people; Voltaire, still more vast, represented Man. Those powerful writers disappeared, but they left us their soul, the Revolution.

Voltaire alone, I repeat it, declared war against that coalition of all the social iniquities, against that enormous and terrible world, and he accepted battle with it.

And what was his weapon? That which has the lightness of the wind and the power of the thunder-bolt. A pen.

With that weapon he fought; with that weapon he conquered.

One of the characteristics which distinguish men of genius from ordinary minds is that they have a double reflection, just as the carbuncle, according to Jerome Cardan, differs from crystal and glass in having a double refraction....

This phenomenon of double reflection raises to the highest power in men of genius what rhetoricians call antithesis, that is to say, the sovereign faculty of seeing the two sides of things.

One of the characteristics of genius is the singular union of faculties the most distant. To draw an astragal like Ariosto, then to dive into souls like Pascal, such is the poet. Man's inner conscience belongs to Shakespeare; he surprises you with it constantly. He extracts from conscience every unforeseen contingence that it contains. Few poets surpass him in this psychical research. Many of the strangest peculiarities of the human mind are indicated by him. He skilfully makes us feel the simplicity of the metaphysical fact under the complication of the dramatic fact.

VICTOR HUGO

A poet must at the same time, and necessarily, be an historian and a philosopher. Herodotus and Thales are included in Homer. Shakespeare, likewise, is this triple man. He is, besides, the painter, and what a painter! — the colossal painter. The poet in reality does more than relate, he exhibits. Poets have in them a reflector, observation, and a condenser, emotion: thence those grand luminous spectres which burst out from their brain, and which go on blazing for ever on the gloomy human wall. These phantoms have life. To exist as much as Achilles would be the ambition of Alexander. Shakespeare has tragedy, comedy, fairyland, hymn, farce, grand divine laughter, terror and horror, and, to say all in one word, the drama. He touches the two poles. He belongs to Olympus and to the traveling booth. No possibility fails him.

The poet is only limited by his aim; he considers nothing but the idea to be worked out; he does not recognise any other sovereignty, any other necessity but the idea; for, art emanating from the absolute, in art, as in the absolute, the end justifies the means.... In art, above all, is visible the *quid divinum*. The poet moves in his work as providence in its own; he excites, astounds, strikes, then exalts or depresses, often in inverse ratio to what you expected, diving into your soul through surprise.

Shakespeare is fertility, force, exuberance, the overflowing breast, the foaming cup, the brimful tub, the overrunning sap, the overflooding lava, the whirlwind scattering germs, the universal rain of life, everything by thousands, everything by millions, no reticence, no binding, no economy, the inordinate and tranquil prodigality of the creator. To those who feel the bottom of their pocket, the inexhaustible seems insane. Will it stop soon? Never. Shakespeare is the sower of dazzling wonders. At every turn, the image; at every turn, contrast; at every turn, light and darkness.

The poet, we have said, is nature. Subtle, minute, keen, microscopical like nature; immense. Not discreet, not reserved, not sparing. Simply magnificent. Let us explain this word, simple.

Sobriety in poetry is poverty; simplicity is grandeur. To give to each thing the quantity of space which fits it, neither more nor less, is simplicity. Simplicity is justice. The whole law of taste is in that. Each thing put in its place and spoken with its own word. On the only condition that a certain latent equilibrium is maintained and a certain mysterious proportion preserved, simplicity may be found in the most stupendous complication, either in the style, or in the *ensemble*. These are the arcana of great art.

JEAN DE LA FONTAINE

Four friends [Molière, Boileau, Racine, and La Fontaine], whose acquaintance had begun at the foot of Parnassus, held a sort of society, which I should call an Academy, if their number had been sufficiently great, and if they had had as much regard for the Muses as for pleasure. The first thing which they did was to banish from among them all rules of conversation, and every thing which savors of the academic conference. When they met, and had sufficiently discussed their amusements, if chance threw them upon any point of science or belles-lettres, they profited by the occasion; it was, however, without dwelling too long on the same subject, flitting from one thing to another like the bees that meet divers sorts of flowers on their way. Neither envy, malice, nor cabal had any voice among them. They adored the works of the ancients, never refused due praise to those of the moderns, spoke modestly of their own, and gave each other sincere counsel, when any one of them — which rarely happened — fell into the malady of the age, and published a book.

PIERRE LOTI

I have written pages, many and long, about Tahiti; in them there are endless details, even as to the appearance of the tiniest plants — the physiognomy of its mosses.

You may read it all with the best will in the world, — well, and then — do you understand? No — not in the least. Has this helped you to hear, at night, on the Polynesian shores white with coral — to hear, at night, the plaintive sound of the *vivo* (the reed pipe), from the very depth of the woods? or the distant bellowing of conch-shell trumpets?

I was to cross many years of hesitations, of errors, of struggles; to mount many calvaries; to pay cruelly for having been brought up as an isolated sensitive plant; by force of will, to recast and to harden my physical constitution, as well as my moral one — up to that day when, towards my twenty-seven years, a manager of a circus, after having seen how my muscles unbent now like springs of steel, let fall in his admiration these words, the most profound that I may have heard in my life: 'What a pity, sir, that your education may have been begun so late!'

JEAN BAPTISTE POQUELIN MOLIÈRE

PREFACE TO 'TARTUFFE'

Here is a comedy about which much noise has been made; which was persecuted for years, while the persons it ridicules proved that they were much stronger in France than those I had hitherto laughed at. The marquises, the learned women, the luckless husbands, and the doctors had meekly borne their representation; in fact, they made believe to be amused, with the rest of the world, by the portraits made of them. But the hypocrites cannot bear ridicule. They were alarmed at once; and thought it monstrous that I should dare to make fun of their cant and attempt to decry a trade which so many honest folk are concerned in. That was a crime they could not pardon; and they all armed themselves against my comedy with dreadful fury.

If any one will take pains to examine my comedy candidly, he will see that my intentions are wholly innocent; that the play does not, in any sense, laugh at those things which we ought to revere; that I have treated my subject with the precautions which its delicacy required; and that I have used all the art and all the care I possibly could in distinguishing the character of the hypocrite from that of truly pious men. For this very purpose, I employed two whole acts in preparing the way for my scoundrel. The audience is not kept for one moment in doubt; he is known for what he is from the start; and, from end to end, he does not say one word, he does not do one act, which will not show to the spectators the nature of a bad man, and bring into relief that of the good man to which I oppose him.

I know that these gentlemen insinuate, by way of answer, that the theatre is not the place to discuss these matters; but I ask, with all due deference to them, on what they base their theory. It is a proposition which they simply suppose; they have not tried to prove it in any way. It would not be difficult to prove to them, on the other hand, that comedy, among the ancients, had its origin in religion and made part of its Mysteries; that our neighbors the Spaniards never celebrate a church festival in which comedy does not take part; that even among ourselves, it owes its birth to the help of a religious fraternity who still own the Hôtel de Bourgogne, a place formerly set apart to represent the most important Mysteries of our faith; that we may still read comedies written in black-letter by a doctor of the Sorbonne; and finally, to go no farther, that in our own time the sacred plays of Monsieur de Corneille have been acted, to the admiration of all France.

If the purpose of comedy is to correct the vices of men, I do not see why some comedies should be privileged to do so, others not. To allow this would produce results far more dangerous to the State than any other. We have evidence that the stage has great virtue as a public corrective. But the finest shafts of serious morality are often less effective than those of satire; nothing corrects the majority of men so well as a picture of their faults. The strongest means of attacking vice is by exposing it to the laughter of the world. We can endure reproof, but we cannot endure ridicule. We are willing to be wicked, but not to be absurd.

I am reproached for putting pious language into the

mouth of my impostor. Hey! how could I help it, if I truly represented the character of a hypocrite? It is enough, I think, to have made quite clear the criminal motives which make him say these things. I have cut out all sacred terms which might be painful when used by him in a shocking way.

Now, inasmuch as we ought to discuss things, not words, and most of our contradictions come from not understanding each other and using the same words to cover opposite meanings, we have only to strip off the veil of ambiguity and look at what comedy really is, to see whether or not it is condemnable. We shall discover, I think, that, being neither more nor less than a witty poem, reproving the faults of men by agreeable lessons, it cannot be censured without great injustice. If we are willing to listen to the testimony of antiquity, it will tell us that the most celebrated philosophers praised comedy, even those who made profession of austere virtue and rebuked incessantly the vices of their age. It will show us that Aristotle devoted his evenings to the theatre, and took pains to reduce to precepts the art of writing comedy. It will also inform us that its greatest men, the first in dignity, made it their glory to write plays themselves; while others did not disdain to recite in public those they wrote; that Greece paid homage to the art by glorious prizes and the splendid theatres with which she honored it; and that in Rome the art was welcomed with extraordinary honors, — I do not mean in debauched and licentious Rome, under its emperors, but in the disciplined old Rome, under its consuls, in the days when Roman virtue was vigorous.

I will admit that there are places it were better to frequent than the theatre. If blame must indeed be cast on all things that do not look directly toward God, the stage must be one of them; and I should not complain were it condemned with all the rest. But let us suppose — what is true — that the exercises of religion must have intervals, and that men have need of relaxation and amusement; then I maintain that none more innocent can be found than that of comedy.

But I am writing too much. I will end with the remark of a great prince on the comedy of *Tartuffe*.

Eight days after it was forbidden, a play was acted before the court entitled *Hermit Scaramouche*, and the king, as he went out, said to the great prince whom I have mentioned: 'I should like to know why the persons who are so scandalized at Molière's comedy have never said a word against *Scaramouche*.' To which the prince replied: 'The reason is that the comedy of *Scaramouche* laughs at heaven and religion, about which those gentlemen care nothing at all; but Molière's comedy laughs at them; and that is a thing they cannot endure.'

MICHEL DE MONTAIGNE

Language gains in value not so much by being handled and used by vigorous minds, not so much from innovations, as by being put to more forcible and various service, stretching it and bending it; they do not bring words to it but they enrich those they use; they give weight and force to their signification and their use, teaching the language unwonted action, but discreetly and dexterously. But how little this agility is given to all men is seen in so many French writers of this age. They are bold enough and scornful enough not to follow the common path; but lack of invention and discretion is their undoing. There is seen in them only a miserable affectation of singularity, feeble and absurd dissimulations which, instead of uplifting, debase the subject. Provided they can pride themselves on novelty, they care nothing for its effectiveness; to lay hold of a new word, they forsake the usual one, often stronger and more pithy.

I find material enough in our language, but some failure in fashioning it, for there is nothing that might not be done with the terms of hunting and of war, which is a fruitful soil to borrow from; and forms of speech, like plants, are improved and strengthened by transplanting. I find it sufficiently copious, but not sufficiently pliable and vigorous; it usually succumbs under a powerful conception. If you are hard pressed, you often perceive that it weakens and bends beneath you, and that in its default the Latin comes to your aid, and to others Greek. Of some of these words which I have just selected we perceive the force with greater difficulty because usage and familiarity have in some sort cheapened their charm to us and made it commonplace; as in our ordinary speech, there are to be found excellent phrases and metaphors of which the beauty withers with age and the color is tarnished by too general handling. But this takes nothing from their relish for those who have good perception, nor does it lessen the glory of those ancient authors who, it is probable, first used these words with brilliancy.

Men of learning treat these things with too great refinement, in an artificial manner, different from the common and natural one. My page makes love and understands it; read him Léon Hébreu and Ficino; they speak of him, of his thoughts and his acts, and yet he understands nothing of what they say. I do not recognise in Aristotle the greater part of my ordinary emotions; they have been covered and clothed in a different garment, to be worn by his school. God help them! Were I of the profession, I would naturalise art as much as they artificialise nature.

To carry out this purpose of mine, it also suits well that I should write in my own house, in an uncivilised region, where no one assists me or stimulates me, where I seldom meet a man who understands the Latin of his

Pater Noster and who does not know French even less. I should have done it better elsewhere, but the work would have been less mine; and its chief aim and perfection is to be precisely mine. I should rightly correct an accidental error, of which, since I hasten on heedlessly, I am full; but the imperfections which are common and constant in me it would be disloyal to remove. When some one has said to me, or I have said to myself: 'You make too much use of figures of speech; there you have a word of Gascon growth; there you have a hazardous expression' (I eschew none of those that are used on the French streets; they who think to combat usage with grammar make fools of themselves); 'there you have an ignorant remark; there a paradoxical one; this other is too simple'; 'you often play a part; it will be thought that you say in earnest what you say in an assumed character,'... 'Yes,' I answer, 'but I correct heedless errors, not those of habit. Do I not commonly talk thus? Does not this represent me to the life? Enough. I have done what I desired to do: every one recognises me in my book and my book in me.'

JEAN BAPTISTE RACINE

You seem by your letter to envy Mad. C. because she has read more plays and romances than you have. I will give you my sentiments on that head, with the sincerity which it is my duty to use towards you. I am very sorry you lay so much stress on such trifles, which at best should serve only to unbend the mind sometimes, but by no means to engross so much of the heart as I fear they do of yours: you are employed in serious studies, which ought to engage your whole attention; and while thus employed, and we pay masters to instruct you, you should carefully avoid whatever tends to dissipate the mind, and turn you from those studies. Not only conscience and religion oblige you to this conduct, but you should have consideration and respect enough for me, to conform a little to my sentiments, while you are of an age in which you ought to be directed. I do not say that you should not sometimes, by way of amusement, read such things; and you see I have myself many French books very capable of diverting you; but I should be much afflicted if this kind of reading should create in you a disgust for more useful learning....

I have lately read over again, for, I suppose, the hundredth time, the epistles of Cicero to his friends; and I wish at your leisure hours you would read some of them to the ambassador; I am certain they would please him, as, without flattery, I know none who has better caught his manner of writing than he has, whether seriously on great affairs, or jesting agreeably on trifles; in this last kind I think Voiture much beneath either of them. Read the epistles *ad Trebatium, ad Marium, ad*

Papirium Paetum, and others which I will point out to you, whenever you will read; also that from Cælius to Cicero, and you will be astonished to see a man equally gay and eloquent as Cicero. But to form a right judgment, you should familiarize yourself to these letters, by a thorough knowledge of the history of those times, in which Plutarch's *Lives* will assist you. I advise you to purchase the epistles by Grevius, in Holland, octavo; they are excellent reading for a man who is to write letters, whether on business or on less serious subjects.

JEAN JACQUES ROUSSEAU

I have entered upon a performance which is without example, whose accomplishment will have no imitator. I mean to present my fellow-mortals with a man in all the integrity of nature; and this man shall be myself.

I know my heart, and have studied mankind; I am not made like any one I have been acquainted with, perhaps like no one in existence; if not better, I at least claim originality, and whether Nature did wisely in breaking the mould with which she formed me can only be determined after having read this work.

... I daily read... with an avidity and taste uncommon, perhaps unprecedented at my age.

Plutarch presently became my greatest favorite. The

satisfaction I derived from repeated readings I gave this author, extinguished my passion for romances, and I shortly preferred Agesilaus, Brutus, and Aristides, to Orondates, Artemenes, and Juba. These interesting studies, seconded by the conversations they frequently occasioned with my father, produced that republican spirit and love of liberty, that haughty and invincible turn of mind, which rendered me impatient of restraint or servitude, and became the torment of my life, as I continually found myself in situations incompatible with these sentiments. Incessantly occupied with Rome and Athens; conversing, if I may so express myself, with their illustrious heroes; born the citizen of a republic, of a father whose ruling passion was a love of his country, I was fired with these examples; could fancy myself a Greek or Roman, and readily give into the character of the personage whose life I read; transported by the recital of any extraordinary instance of fortitude or intrepidity, animation flashed from my eyes, and gave my voice additional strength and energy.

One day I took the *Mercure de France*, and as I walked and read, I came to the following question proposed by the academy of Dijon, for the premium of the ensuing year, *Has the progress of sciences and arts contributed to corrupt or purify morals?*

The moment I had read this, I seemed to behold another world, and became a different man. Although

I have a lively remembrance of the impression it made upon me, the detail has escaped my mind, since I communicated it to M. de Malesherbes in one of my four letters to him. This is one of the singularities of my memory which merits to be remarked. It serves me in proportion to my dependence upon it; the moment I have committed to paper that with which it was charged, it forsakes me, and I have no sooner written a thing than I had forgotten it entirely. This singularity is the same with respect to music. Before I learned the use of notes I knew a great number of songs; the moment I had made a sufficient progress to sing an air set to music, I could not recollect any one of them; and at present, I much doubt whether I should be able entirely to go through one of those of which I was the most fond. All I distinctly recollect upon this occasion is, that on my arrival at Vincennes, I was in an agitation which approached a delirium. Diderot perceived it; I told him the cause, and read to him the prosopopœia of Fabricius, written with a pencil under a tree. He encouraged me to pursue my ideas, and to become a competitor for the premium. I did so, and from that moment I was ruined.

All the rest of my misfortunes during my life were the inevitable effect of this moment of error.

My sentiments became elevated with the most inconceivable rapidity to the level of my ideas. All my little passions were stifled by the enthusiasm of truth, liberty, and virtue; and, what is most astonishing, this effervescence continued in my mind upwards of five years, to as great a degree perhaps as it has ever done in that of any other man. I composed the discourse in a very singular manner, and in that style which I have always followed in my other works. I dedicated to it the hours of the night in which sleep deserted me, I meditated in my bed with my eyes closed, and in my mind turned over and over again my periods with incredible labor and care; the moment they were finished to my satisfaction, I deposited them in my memory, until I had an opportunity of committing them to paper; but the time of rising and putting on my clothes made me lose everything, and when I took up my pen I recollected but little of what I had composed. I made Madame le Vasseur my secretary; I had lodged her with her daughter, and husband, nearer to myself; and she, to save me the expense of a servant, came every morning to make my fire, and to do such other little things as were necessary. As soon as she arrived I dictated to her while in bed what I had composed in the night, and this method, which for a long time I observed, preserved me many things I should otherwise have forgotten.

As soon as the discourse was finished, I showed it to Diderot. He was satisfied with the production, and pointed out some corrections he thought necessary to be made. However, this composition, full of force and fire, absolutely wants logic and order; of all the works I ever wrote, this is the weakest in reasoning, and the most devoid of number and harmony. With whatever talent a man may be born, the art of writing is not easily learned.

CHARLES AUGUSTIN SAINTE-BEUVE
WHAT IS A CLASSIC?

A delicate question, to which somewhat diverse solutions might be given according to times and seasons. An intelligent man suggests it to me, and I intend to try, if not to solve it, at least to examine and discuss it face to face with my readers, were it only to persuade them to answer it for themselves, and, if I can, to make their opinion and mine on the point clear. And why, in criticism, should we not, from time to time, venture to treat some of those subjects which are not personal, in which we no longer speak of some one but of some thing? Our neighbors, the English, have well succeeded in making of it a special division of literature under the modest title of 'Essays.' It is true that in writing of such subjects always slightly abstract and moral it is advisable to speak of them in a season of quiet, to make sure of our own attention and of that of others, to seize one of those moments of calm moderation and leisure seldom granted our amiable France; even when she is desirous of being wise and is not making revolutions, her brilliant genius can scarcely tolerate them.

A classic, according to the usual definition, is an old author canonized by admiration, and an authority in his particular style. The word classic was first used in this sense by the Romans. With them not all the citizens of the different classes were properly called *classici*, but only those of the chief class, those who possessed an income of a certain fixed sum. Those who possessed a smaller income were described by the term *infra classem*, below the preëminent class. The word *classicus* was used in a figurative sense by Aulus Gellius, and applied to writers: a writer of worth and distinction, *classicus assiduusque scriptor*, a writer who is of account, has real property, and is not lost in the proletariate crowd. Such an expression implies an age sufficiently advanced to have already made some sort of valuation and classification of literature.

A true classic, as I should like to hear it defined, is an author who has enriched the human mind, increased its treasure, and caused it to advance a step; who has discovered some moral and not equivocal truth, or revealed some eternal passion in that heart where all seemed known and discovered; who has expressed his thought, observation, or invention, in no matter what form, only provided it be broad and great, refined and sensible, sane and beautiful in itself; who has spoken to all in his own peculiar style, a style which is found to be also that of the whole world, a style new without neologism, new and old, easily contemporary with all time.

Such a classic may for a moment have been revolutionary; it may at least have seemed so, but it is not; it only lashed and subverted whatever prevented the restoration of the balance of order and beauty.

If it is desired, names may be applied to this definition, which I wish to make purposely majestic and fluctuating, or in a word, all-embracing. I should first put there Corneille of the *Polyeucte*, *Cinna*, and *Horaces*. I should put Molière there, the fullest and most complete poetic genius we have ever had in France. Goethe, the king of critics, said: 'Molière is so great that he astonishes us afresh every time we read him. He is a man apart; his plays border on the tragic, and no one has the courage to try and imitate him. His *Avare*, where vice destroys all affections between father and son, is one of the most sublime works, and dramatic in the highest degree. In a drama every action ought to be important in itself, and to lead to an action greater still. In this respect *Tartuffe* is a model. What a piece of exposition the first scene is! From the beginning everything has an important meaning, and causes something much more important to be foreseen. The exposition in a certain play of Lessing that might be mentioned is very fine, but the world only sees that of *Tartuffe* once. It is the finest of the kind we possess. Every year I read a play of Molière, just as from time to time I contemplate some engraving after the great Italian masters.'

I do not conceal from myself that the definition of the classic I have just given somewhat exceeds the notion usually ascribed to the term. It should, above all, include conditions of uniformity, wisdom, moderation, and reason, which dominate and contain all the others. Having to praise M. Royer-Collard, M. de Rémusat said — 'If he derives purity of taste, propriety of terms, variety of expression, attentive care in suiting the diction to the thought, from our classics, he owes to himself alone the distinctive character he gives it all.' It is here evident that the part allotted to classical qualities seems mostly to depend on harmony and nuances of expression, on graceful and temperate style: such is also the most general opinion. In this sense the preëminent classics would be writers of a middling order, exact, sensible, elegant, always clear, yet of noble feeling and airily veiled strength.

The important point now seems to me to be to uphold, while extending, the idea and belief. There is no receipt for making classics; this point should be clearly recognized. To believe that an author will become a classic by imitating certain qualities of purity, moderation, accuracy, and elegance, independently of the style and inspiration, is to believe that after Racine the father there is a place for Racine the son; dull and estimable rôle, the worst in poetry. Further, it is hazardous to make too quickly and without opposition the place of a classic in the sight of one's contemporaries; in that case there is a good chance of not retaining the position with posterity.

There comes a time in life, when, all our journeys over, our experiences ended, there is no enjoyment more delightful than to study and thoroughly examine the things we know, to take pleasure in what we feel, and in seeing and seeing again the people we love: the pure joys of our maturity. Then it is that the word classic takes its true meaning, and is defined for every man of taste by an irresistible choice. Then taste is formed, it is shaped and definite; then good sense, if we are to possess it at all, is perfected in us. We have neither more time for experiments, nor a desire to go forth in search of pastures new. We cling to our friends, to those proved by a long intercourse. Old wine, old books, old friends. We say to ourselves with Voltaire in these delightful lines: 'Let us enjoy, let us write, let us live, my dear Horace!... I have lived longer than you: my verse will not last so long. But on the brink of the tomb I shall make it my chief care — to follow the lessons of your philosophy — to despise death in enjoying life — to read your writings full of charm and good sense — as we drink an old wine which revives our senses.'

GEORGE SAND

To the younger Dumas

Try to keep your soul young and quivering right up to old age, and to imagine right up to the brink of death that life is only beginning. I think that is the only way to keep adding to one's talent, to one's affections, and one's inner happiness.

To Flaubert

Keep your excessive regard for form, but do take more trouble about the foundations. Do not take real quality to be an inevitable accompaniment of impeccable form.

One ought to write for every one who has any desire to read and can take advantage of good books.

You say M. Flaubert would be lacking in manners if he were to allow his thought and his literary aim to be evident. That is false, false as hell!

From the moment that M. Flaubert begins to write well and seriously one becomes attached to his personality and desires to be lost or saved with him.

However hard you struggle, your story cannot be anything but a conversation between author and readers.

To Flaubert

Nohant, 28th October, 1867

I have just written my impressions of the Normandy landscape in a few pages; it is nothing of importance, but I was able to bring in three lines of *Salammbô* between inverted commas which appeared to me to paint the countryside better than all my phrases, lines which have always struck me like a magisterial stroke of the brush. Turning over the pages of *Salammbô* to find those lines, I naturally re-read almost the whole book, and I remain convinced that it is one of the most beautiful books which has ever been written since books have been written at all.

To Flaubert

Nohant, 31 December, 1867

... I think an artist ought to live according to his own nature so far as it is possible. Then let the fighter fight, and the lover, love; while an aging artist like myself loves nature, travel, botany, and geology, and children and family life, and everything which moves one's heart, and combats moral anæmia.

I think that art needs a palette always overflowing with tender or violent colors according to the subject of the picture; that the artist is an instrument which should be played upon by all, before he can play upon others, but all that is perhaps not applicable to a spirit of your type, which has already acquired much sustenance and has only to digest it. I shall only insist upon one point, which is that the physical being is entirely necessary to the moral being, and that I fear a breakdown in health for you some time or another, which will force you to stop your work and leave it to get cold.

To Flaubert

Paris, August, 1868

... The difficulties of producing a play have to be seen to be believed, and if one does not fit on a breastplate of humor and inner gaiety in the study of human nature, there is enough to make you *rage against* it. But I have long given up raging. I laugh instead. It is all too deadly familiar to me to move me now and I shall have some funny stories to tell you when we meet.

To Flaubert

Nohant, 21 December, 1868

... Turgeniev was more fortunate than me, since he was able to tear you from your inkpot. I know him personally only a very little, but I know his books by heart. What a talent! And what an absolute original! I think foreign writers have a better way with them than we have. They never pose, and we either drape ourselves with our dignity, or make an exhibition of ourselves. The Frenchman has neither a social nor an intellectual circle nowadays.

I except you, who live an exceptional life, and I except myself because of the stratum of gipsy insouciance in the depths of my being which has been bestowed on me. But then I admit that I cannot polish and repolish my work; *I love life too much and am too much occupied with the mustard and pickles of life, as opposed to the solid fare, ever to be a real woman of letters.* I have had fits of it certainly; but it has not lasted. Existence in which one can drown one's ego and forget all about it, is so very good, and life in which one is not playing any part is such a jolly play to see! When I *have* to give out my personal force, I live on courage and resolution, but I do not enjoy the process.

As for you, crazy troubadour, I suspect you of caring more for the writer's trade than for anything else in the world. In spite of what you say, it might well be true that *art* is your only passion, and that your monastic life, which always touches my heart, fool that I am, is your idea of bliss. If that is so, all the better, but admit it to console me.

FRANÇOIS MARIE AROUET DE VOLTAIRE
To M. Helvétius

Cirey, February 25, 1739

My dear friend — the friend of Truth and the Muses — your *Epistle* is full of bold reasoning in advance of your age, and still more in advance of those craven writers who rhyme for the booksellers and restrict themselves within the compass of a royal censor, who is either jealous of them, or more cowardly than they are themselves.

What are they but miserable birds, with their wings close clipped, who, longing to soar, are for ever falling back to earth, breaking their legs! You have a fearless genius, and your work sparkles with imagination. I much prefer your generous faults to the mediocre prettinesses with which we are cloyed. If you will allow me to tell you where I think you can improve yourself in your art, I should say: Beware, lest in attempting the grand, you overshoot the mark and fall into the grandiose: only employ true similes: and be sure always to use exactly the right word.

Shall I give you an infallible little rule for verse? Here it is. When a thought is just and noble, something still remains to be done with it: see if the way you have expressed it in verse would be effective in prose: and if your verse, without the swing of the rhyme, seems to you to have a word too many — if there is the least defect in the construction — if a conjunction is forgotten — if, in brief, the right word is not used, or not used in the right place, you must then conclude that the jewel of your thought is not well set. Be quite sure that lines which have any one of these faults will never be learnt by heart, and never re-read: and the only good verses are those which one re-reads and remembers, in spite of oneself. There are many of this kind in your *Epistle* — lines which no one else in this generation can write at your age — such as were written fifty years ago.

Do not be afraid, then, to bring your talents to Parnassus; they will undoubtedly redound to your credit because you never neglect your duties for them: they are themselves very pleasant duties. Surely, those your position demands of you must be very uncongenial to such a nature as yours. They are as much routine as looking after a house, or the housebook of one's steward. Why should you be deprived of liberty of thought because you happen to be a farmer-general? Atticus was a farmer-general, the old Romans were farmers-general, and they thought — as Romans. Go ahead, Atticus.

CRITICISING A CRITIC

To M. Martin Kahle

I am very pleased to hear, sir, that you have written a little book against me. You do me too much honour. On page 17 you reject the proof, from final causes, of the existence of God. If you had argued thus at Rome, the reverend father and governor of the Holy Palace would have condemned you to the Inquisition: if you had written thus against a theologian of Paris, he would have had your proposition censured by the sacred faculty: if against a devout person, he would have abused you: but I have the honour to be neither a Jesuit, nor a theologian, nor a devotee. I shall leave you to your opinion, and shall remain of mine. I shall always be convinced that a watch proves a watchmaker, and that the universe proves a God. I hope that you yourself understand what you say concerning space and eternity, the necessity of matter, and preordained harmony: and I recommend you to look once more at what *I* said, finally, in the new edition, where I earnestly endeavoured to make myself thoroughly understood — and in metaphysics that is no easy task.

You quote, apropos of space and infinity, the *Medea* of Seneca, the *Philippics* of Cicero, and the *Metamorphoses* of Ovid; also the verses of the Duke of Buckingham, of Gombauld, Regnier, and Rapin. I must tell you, sir, I know at least as much poetry as you do: that I am quite as fond of it: that if it comes to capping verses we shall see some very pretty sport: only I do not think them suitable to shed light on a metaphysical question, be they Lucretius' or the Cardinal de Polignac's.

Furthermore, if ever you understand anything about preordained harmony — if you discover how, under the law of necessity, man is free — you will do me a service if you will pass on the information to me. When you have shown, in verse or otherwise, why so many men cut their throats in the best of all possible worlds, I shall be exceedingly obliged to you.

I await your arguments, your verses, and your abuse: and assure you from the bottom of my heart that neither you nor I know anything about the matter.

For if morality is the aim of poetry, I do not apprehend why the poet should be forbidden to intersperse his descriptions with moral sentences and useful reflexions, provided he scatters them with a sparing hand, and in proper places, either when he wants personages to utter those thoughts, or when their character does not permit them to speak in the behalf of virtue.

A poem, methinks, might subsist very well, without the help of mechanick, or anatomical descriptions. We rather require of an author, to excite our passions, to unfold the most intricate recesses of the soul, to describe the customs of the nations, to mark the differences which arise in the characters of men, from the different governments they are born under, in short to speak the language of the polite world; than to play the surgeon, the carpenter, or the joiner, though never so elegantly.

GERMAN WRITERS
JOHANN WOLFGANG VON GOETHE

To Carlyle

It is obvious that the efforts of the best poets and æsthetic writers of all nations have now for some time been directed towards what is universal in humanity. In each special field, whether in history, mythology, or fiction, more or less arbitrarily conceived, one sees the traits which are universal always more clearly revealed and illumining what is merely national and personal.

Though something of the same sort prevails now also in practical life, pervading all that is earthy, crude, wild, cruel, false, selfish, and treacherous, and striving to diffuse everywhere some gentleness, we cannot indeed hope that universal peace is being ushered in thereby, but only that inevitable strife will be gradually more restrained, war will become less cruel, and victory less insolent.

Whatever in the poetry of any nation tends to this and contributes to it, the others should endeavour to appropriate. The peculiarities of each nation must be learned, and allowance made for them, in order by these very means to hold intercourse with it; for the special characteristics of a nation are like its language and its currency: they facilitate intercourse, nay they first make it completely possible.

A genuine, universal tolerance is most surely attained,

if we do not quarrel with the peculiar characteristics of individual men and races, but only hold fast the conviction, that what is truly excellent is distinguished by its belonging to all mankind. To such intercourse and mutual recognition, the German people have long contributed.

Whoever understands and studies German finds himself in the market, where all nations offer their wares; he plays the interpreter, while he enriches himself.

And thus every translator is to be regarded as a middleman in this universal spiritual commerce, and as making it his business to promote this exchange: for say what we may of the insufficiency of translation, yet the work is and will always be one of the weightiest and worthiest affairs in the general concerns of the world.

The Koran says: 'God had given to each people a prophet in its own tongue!' Thus each translator is a prophet to his people. Luther's translation of the Bible has produced the greatest results, though criticism gives it qualified praise, and picks faults in it, even to the present day. What indeed is the whole enormous business of the Bible Society, but to make known the Gospel to all people in their own tongue?

HEINRICH HEINE

When one has too much to write to people, one ceases to write altogether; but necessity compels me to take up my pen today.... I must give your style the highest praise. I am a competent judge of style — only, on your life, do not grow careless and do not cease to study the turns of speech, and the framing of words of Lessing, Luther, Goethe, Varnhagen, and H. Heine; may God preserve this last classic!

I need solitude for my work; a number of annoying adventures have prevented my writing a single intelligent word in the last four weeks; and I am constrained to end my life — the written one.

My most important work is my Memoirs, but they will not appear soon. I should like best for them to be published after my death!

But tell me what is the fundamental reason for the curse which falls upon all men of great genius? Why does the lightning of unhappiness strike most often the lofty spirits, the towers of humanity, while it so compassionately spares the humble thatched roofs of mediocrity?

I am trying to fortify my mind for the future; not long ago I read the whole of Shakespeare, and now, by the sea, I am reading the Bible. As for public opinion of my earlier writings it depends so much upon such a sequence and concurrence of things that I cannot have much to do with it myself. But I do honestly confess that the great interests of European life always interest me far more than my own books — *que Dieu les prenne en sa sainte et digne garde!*

To Alexandre Dumas

I have been bed-ridden for six years. In the worst hours of my illness, when I was in the greatest agony, my wife used to read aloud your romances, and that was the only thing that could make me forget my suffering.

I devoured them all, and as they were read aloud I used often to cry out: 'What a gifted poet is this great boy called Alexandre Dumas!'

Truly, after Cervantes and Madame Schariar, known by the name of the Sultana Scheherazade, you are the most entertaining story-teller I know.

Strange, after having passed the whole of my life in gliding about the dancing floors of philosophy, and abandoning myself to all the orgies of the intellect, and dallying with systems without ever being satisfied — I have suddenly arrived at the same point of view as Uncle Tom, taking my stand on the Bible and kneeling beside my black brother in prayer in the same act of devotion.

I have, as they say, done nothing in this lovely world. I have become nothing, nothing but a poet.

No; I will not succumb to hypocritical humility and disparage that title. A man who is a poet is much, and much if he is a great lyric poet in Germany, in the nation which has surpassed all others in two things — philosophy and song. I will not deny my fame as a poet with false modesty, the invention of rascals. None of my compatriots has won his laurels so easily as I...

Ah! Fame, that gew-gaw once so sweet, sweet as pine-apples and flattery, has been spoiled for me for long enough; it is as bitter to me now as wormwood. I can say like Romeo: 'I am Fortune's fool.' I stand now before the great tureen, but I have no spoon. What does it boot me that my health is drunk in the best wines from golden goblets at banquets, when I myself, cut off from all the pleasures of the world, can only moisten my lips with a thin gruel?

GOTTHOLD EPHRAIM LESSING

'When a poetaster,' says Horace, 'can do nothing else, he falls to describing a grove, an altar, a brook winding through pleasant meadows, a rushing river, or a rainbow.'

Pope, when a man, looked back with contempt on the descriptive efforts of his poetic childhood. He expressly enjoined upon every one, who would not prove himself unworthy the name of poet, to abandon as early as possible this fondness for description. A merely descriptive poem he declared to be a feast made up of sauces.

Painting and poetry should be like two just and friendly neighbors, neither of whom indeed is allowed to take unseemly liberties in the heart of the other's domain, but who exercise mutual forbearance on the borders, and effect a peaceful settlement for all the petty encroachments which circumstances may compel either to make in haste on the rights of the other.

Paint us, ye poets, the delight, the attraction, the love, the enchantment of beauty, and you have painted beauty itself....

Yet another way in which poetry surpasses art in the description of physical beauty, is by turning beauty into charm. Charm is beauty in motion, and therefore less adapted to the painter than the poet. The painter can suggest motion, but his figures are really destitute of it. Charm therefore in a picture becomes grimace, while in poetry it remains what it is, a transitory beauty, which we would fain see repeated.

FRIEDRICH NIETZSCHE

Has any one at the end of the nineteenth century any distinct notion of what poets of a stronger age understood by the word inspiration? If not, I will describe it. If one had the smallest vestige of superstition in one, it would hardly be possible to set aside completely the idea that one is the mere incarnation, mouthpiece or medium of an almighty power. The idea of revelation in the sense that something becomes suddenly visible and audible with indescribable certainty and accuracy, which profoundly convulses and upsets one — describes simply the matter of fact.... Everything happens quite involuntarily, as if in a tempestuous outburst of freedom, of absoluteness, of power and divinity. The involuntariness of the figures and similes is the most remarkable thing; one loses all perception of what constitutes the figure and what constitutes the simile; everything seems to present itself as the readiest, the correctest and the simplest means of expression. It actually seems, to use one of Zarathustra's own phrases, as if all things came unto one, and would fain be similes: 'Here do all things come caressingly to thy talk and flatter thee, for they want to ride upon thy back....'

Of all that is written, I love only what a person hath written with his blood. Write with blood, and thou wilt find that blood is spirit.

It is no easy task to understand unfamiliar blood; I hate the reading idlers.

He who knoweth the reader, doeth nothing more for the reader. Another century of readers — and spirit itself will stink.

Every one being allowed to learn to read, ruineth in the long run not only writing but also thinking.

Once spirit was God, then it became man, and now it even becometh populace.

He that writeth in blood and proverbs doth not want to be read, but learnt by heart.

In the mountains the shortest way is from peak to peak, but for that route thou must have long legs. Proverbs should be peaks, and those spoken to should be big and tall.

JOHANN CHRISTOPH FRIEDRICH VON SCHILLER

But how can the artist protect himself from the corruptions of his age, which on all sides surround him? By despising its judgment. Let him look upwards to his dignity and the law, not downwards to his prosperity and his wants. Alike free from the vain activity, that would fain leave its traces on the fleeting moment, and from the impatient enthusiasm, that applies the scale of the absolute to the paltry product of time, let him leave to the understanding, which is here at home, the sphere of the actual; but let him strive to evolve the ideal from the union of the possible with the necessary. This let him express in fiction and truth, in the play of his fancy and in the gravity of his deeds, in all sensible and spiritual forms, and cast it silently into infinite time.

But every one whose soul glows with this ideal, does not possess the creative tranquillity and patience, to impress it upon the silent stone, or pour it out in sober words, and commit it to the trusty hands of time.

A poet treats his subject in a common way, if he brings out unimportant actions and passes hastily over the important. He treats it in a great way, if he unites it with the Great. Homer knew how to give a spirited treatment to the shield of Achilles, although the material fabrication of a shield is something very common.

The tragic poet will always mar the perfection of his work, if he cannot succeed without introducing a villain, and if he is compelled to deduce greatness of suffering from greatness of crime. Shakspeare's Iago and Lady Macbeth, Cleopatra in Roxolana, Franz Moor in the Robbers, testify for this assertion. A poet, who understands his true interest, will not let misfortune depend upon an evil will which meditates misfortune, nor still less upon a deficiency of intellect, but upon the stress of circumstances. If it does not result from moral sources, but from external things, which neither have a will nor are subject to one, our compassion is purer, and, at least, is not weakened by any representation of moral incongruity. But then the sympathizing spectator is not exempt from the unpleasant feeling of an incongruity in nature, which in this case moral conformity alone can save. Compassion mounts to a degree much higher, if its objects are both him who suffers and him who originates the suffering. This can occur only if the latter excites neither our hatred nor our contempt, but has been brought against his inclination, to become the author of misfortune. Thus it is a preëminent beauty in the German Iphigenia, that the king of Taurus, the only one who opposes the wishes of Orestes and his sister, never forfeits our regard, and even extorts love from us at last.

Then Pathos is the first and indispensable requisite for a tragic artist, and he is allowed to carry the representation of sorrow as far as it can be done, without endangering his *final design*, without suppression of the moral freedom. He must, so to speak, give his hero or his reader the complete freight of sorrow, because otherwise it continues to be problematic, whether his opposition thereto is a mental action, and something *positive*, and not rather something purely *negative*, and a deficiency.

The latter is the case with the old French tragedy, in which we are very seldom or never shown a *suffering nature*, but generally see only cold, declamatory poets, or comedians upon stilts. The frosty tone of declamation extinguishes all true nature, and their adorable *decency* makes it completely impossible for French tragic poets to portray humanity in its truth. Decency falsifies, even in its own proper place, the expression of nature, and yet the art demands the latter imperatively. We can hardly believe it in a French tragic hero, that he *suffers*, for he delivers himself concerning his state of mind, like the calmest of men; and his incessant regard to the impression which he makes upon others, never allows him to leave to his own nature its freedom. The kings, princesses and heroes of a Corneille and Voltaire, never forget their *rank* in the most vehement passion, and they put off their *humanity* far sooner than their *dignity*. They are like the kings and emperors in the old picture-books, who go to bed with their crowns on.

How different with the Greeks, and those of the moderns who have composed in their spirit! The Greek is never ashamed of nature; he allows to the sensuousness its full rights, and yet is always secure from being overcome by it. His deeper and correcter intellect permits him to distinguish the contingent, which a bad taste magnifies, from the necessary. But all in man, that is not humanity, is contingent.

ARTHUR SCHOPENHAUER

Metaphors and *similes* are of great value, in so far as they explain an unknown relation by a known one. Even the more detailed simile which grows into a parable or an allegory, is nothing more than the exhibition of some relation in its simplest, most visible and palpable form. The growth of ideas rests, at bottom, upon similes; because ideas arise by a process of combining the similarities and neglecting the differences between things. Further, intelligence, in the strict sense of the word, ultimately consists in a seizing of relations; and a clear and pure grasp of relations is all the more often attained when the comparison is made between cases that lie wide apart from one another, and between things of quite different nature. As long as a relation is known to me as existing only in a single case, I have but an *individual* idea of it — in other words, only an *intuitive* knowledge of it; but as soon as I see the same relation in two different cases, I have a *general* idea of its whole nature, and this is a deeper and more perfect knowledge.

Since then, similes and metaphors are such a powerful engine of knowledge, it is a sign of great intelligence in a writer if his similes are unusual and, at the same time, to the point. Aristotle also observes that by far the most important thing to a writer is to have this power of metaphor; for it is a gift which cannot be acquired, and it is a mark of genius.

A man's works are the quintessence of his mind, and even though he may possess very great capacity, they will always be incomparably more valuable than his conversation.

Writing for money and reservation of copyright are, at bottom, the ruin of literature. No one writes anything that is worth writing, unless he writes entirely for the sake of his subject.... The best works of the greatest men all come from the time when they had to write for nothing or for very little.

The first rule, then, for a good style is that *the author should have something to say;* nay, this is in itself almost all that is necessary. Ah, how much it means! The neglect of this rule is a fundamental trait in the philosophical writing, and, in fact, in all the reflective literature, of my country, more especially since Fichte.

On the other hand, a good author, fertile in ideas, soon wins his reader's confidence that, when he writes, he has really and truly *something to say;* and this gives the intelligent reader patience to follow him with attention. Such an author, just because he really has something to say, will never fail to express himself in the simplest and most straightforward manner; because his object is to awake the very same thought in the reader that he has in himself, and no other. So he will be able to affirm with Boileau that his thoughts are everywhere open to the light of the day, and that his verse always says something, whether it says it well or ill:

> Ma pensée au grand jour partout s'offre et s'expose,
> Et mon vers, bien ou mal, dit toujours quelque chose.

... Another characteristic of such writers is that they always avoid a positive assertion wherever they can possibly do so, in order to leave a loophole for escape in case of need. Hence they never fail to choose the more *abstract* way of expressing themselves; whereas intelligent people use the more *concrete;* because the latter brings things more within the range of actual demonstration, which is the source of all evidence.

As exaggeration generally produces an effect the opposite of that aimed at; so words, it is true, serve to make thought intelligible — but only up to a certain point. If words are heaped up beyond it, the thought becomes more and more obscure again. To find where the point lies is the problem of style, and the business of the critical faculty; for a word too much always defeats its purpose.

True brevity of expression consists in everywhere saying only what is worth saying, and in avoiding tedious detail about things which every one can supply for himself. This involves correct discrimination between what is necessary and what is superfluous.

To gain *immortality* an author must possess so many excellences that, while it will not be easy to find any one to understand and appreciate them all, there will be men in every age who are able to recognize and value some of them. In this way the credit of his book will be maintained throughout the long course of centuries, in spite of the fact that human interests are always changing.

Again, it may be said that there are three kinds of authors. First come those who write without thinking. They write from a full memory, from reminiscences; it may be, even straight out of other people's books. This class is the most numerous. Then come those who do their thinking whilst they are writing, — they think in order to write; and there is no lack of them. Last of all come those authors who think before they begin to write: they are rare.

Authors of the second class, who put off their thinking until they come to write, are like a sportsman who goes forth at random and is not likely to bring very much home. On the other hand, when an author of the third or rare class writes, it is like a *battue*. Here the game has been previously captured and shut up within a very small space; from which it is afterwards let out, so many at a time, into another space, also confined. The game cannot possibly escape the sportsman; he has nothing to do but aim and fire, — in other words, write down his thoughts. This is a kind of sport from which a man has something to show.

But even though the number of those who really think seriously before they begin to write is small, extremely few of them think about *the subject itself:* the remainder think only about the books that have been written on the subject, and what has been said by others. In order to think at all, such writers need the more direct and powerful stimulus of having other people's thoughts before them. These become their immediate theme; and the result is that they are always under their influence, and so never, in any real sense of the word, original. But the former are roused to thought by the subject itself, to which their thinking is thus immediately directed. This is the only class that produces writers of abiding fame.

It must of course be understood that I am speaking here of writers who treat of great subjects; not of writers on the art of making brandy.

ITALIAN WRITER
DANTE ALIGHIERI

For some words are *childish*, some *feminine*, some *manly:* and of these last some are *sylvan*, others *urban*; and of those we call urban we feel that some are *combed-out* and *glossy*, some *shaggy* and *rumpled*. Now, among these urban words, the combed-out and the shaggy are those we call *grand*; whilst we call the glossy and the rumpled those whose sound is superfluous, just as among great works some are works of magnanimity, others of smoke; and as to these last, although when superficially looked at there may be thought to be a kind of ascent, still (when they are viewed), by sound reason no ascent will be found, but rather a headlong fall down giddy precipices, because the marked-out path of virtue is departed from.

SCANDINAVIAN WRITERS
GEORG BRANDES

He who possesses talent should also possess courage. He must dare trust his inspiration, he must be convinced that the fancy which flashes through his brain is a healthy one, that the form which comes natural to him, even if it be a new one, has a right to assert its claims; he must have gained the hardihood to expose himself to the charge of being affected, or on the wrong path, before he can yield to his instinct and follow it wherever it may imperiously lead. When Armand Carrel, a young journalist at the time, was censured by the editor of the paper for which he wrote, who, pointing to a passage in the young man's article, remarked, 'That is not the way people write,' he replied, 'I do not write as people write, but as I myself write,' and this is the universal formula of a gifted nature. It countenances neither fugitive rubbish, nor arbitrary invention, but with entire self-consciousness it expresses the right of talent, when neither traditional form nor existing material suffices to meet the peculiar requirements of its nature, to choose new material, to create new forms, until it finds a soil of a quality to give nurture to all of its forces and gently and freely develop them. Such a soil the poet Hans Christian Andersen found in the nursery story.

In his stories we meet with beginnings like this: 'Any

one might have supposed that something very extraordinary had happened in the duck-pond, there was such a commotion. All the ducks — some swimming, some standing in the pond with their heads downward — suddenly jumped on land, leaving the traces of their feet in the wet clay, and sending forth a loud, startled cry,' or like the following: 'Now, then, let us begin. When we are at the end of the story, we shall know more than we know now: but to begin. Once upon a time there was a wicked sprite, indeed, he was the most mischievous of all sprites!' The construction, the position of the words in individual sentences, the entire arrangement, is at variance with the simplest rules of syntax. 'This is not the way people write.' That is true; but it is the way they speak. To grown people? No, but to children; and why should it not be proper to commit the words to writing in the same order in which they are spoken to children? In such a case the usual form is simply exchanged for another; not the rules of abstract written language, but the power of comprehension of the child is here the determining factor; there is method in this disorder, as there is method in the grammatical blunder of the child when it makes use of a regular imperfect for an irregular verb. To replace the accepted written language with the free, unrestrained language of familiar conversation, to exchange the more rigid form of expression of grown people for such as a child uses and understands, becomes the true goal of the author as soon as he embraces the resolution to tell nursery stories for children. He has the bold intention to employ oral speech in a printed work, he will not write but speak, and he will gladly write as a school-child writes, if he can thus avoid speaking as a book speaks. The written word is poor and insufficient, the oral has a host of allies in the expression of the mouth that imitates the object to which the discourse relates, in the movement of the hand that describes it, in the length or shortness of the tone of the voice, in its sharp or gentle, grave or droll character, in the entire play of the features, and in the whole bearing. The nearer to a state of nature the being addressed, the greater aids to comprehension are these auxiliaries. Whoever tells a story to a child, involuntarily accompanies the narrative with many gestures and grimaces, for the child sees the story quite as much as it hears it, paying heed, almost in the same way as the dog, rather to the tender or irritated intonation, than to whether the words express friendliness or wrath. Whoever, therefore, addresses himself in writing to a child must have at his command the changeful cadence, the sudden pauses, the descriptive gesticulations, the awe-inspiring mien, the smile which betrays the happy turn of affairs, the jest, the caress, and the appeal to rouse the flagging attention — all these he must endeavor to weave into his diction, and as he cannot directly sing, paint, or dance the occurrences to the child, he must imprison within his prose the song, the picture, and the pantomimic movements, that they may lie there like forces in bonds, and rise up in their might as soon as the book is opened. In the first place, no circumlocution; everything must be spoken fresh from the lips of the narrator, aye, more than spoken, growled, buzzed, and blown as from a trumpet: 'There came a soldier marching along the high-road — *one, two! one, two!*' 'And the carved trumpeters blew, "Trateratra! there is the little boy! Trateratra!"' — '"Listen how it is drumming on the burdock-leaves, rum-dum-dum! rum-dum-dum!" said the Father Snail.' At one time he begins, as in 'The Daisy,' with a 'Now you shall hear!' which at once arrests the attention; and again he jests after the fashion of a child: 'So the soldier cut the witch's head off. There she lay!' We can hear the laughter of the child that follows this brief, not very sympathetic, yet extremely clear presentation of the destruction of an impostor. Often he breaks into a sentimental tone...

HENRIK IBSEN

To Peter Hansen

Dresden, 28th October, 1870

But it is really more the story of my intellectual development that you want. Here it is, then.

Everything which I have created as a poet has had its origin in a frame of mind and a situation in life; I never wrote because I had, as they say, 'found a good subject.'

Now I shall confess chronologically.

Catiline was written in a little provincial town, where it was impossible for me to give expression to all that fermented in me except by mad, riotous pranks, which brought down upon me the ill-will of all the respectable citizens, who could not enter into that world which I was wrestling with alone.

Lady Inger of Östraat is the result of a love-affair — hastily entered into and violently broken off — to which several smaller poems may also be attributed, such as 'Markblomster og potteplanter' (Field-flowers and pot-plants), 'Fuglevise' (A Bird Song), etc., which were printed in the *Nyhedsblad* (and to which I take this opportunity of calling your attention).

The Vikings at Helgeland I wrote whilst I was engaged to be married. For Hjördis I had the same model as I took afterwards for Svanhild in *Love's Comedy.*

Not until I was married did more serious interests take possession of my life. The first outcome of this change was a long poem — 'Paa Vidderne' (On the Heights). The desire for emancipation which pervades this poem did not, however, receive its full expression until I wrote *Love's Comedy*, a book which gave rise to much talk in Norway. People mixed up my personal affairs in the discussion, and I fell greatly in public estimation. The only person at that time who approved of the book was my wife. Hers is exactly the character desiderated by a man of mind — she is illogical, but has a strong poetic instinct, a broad and liberal mind, and an almost violent antipathy to all petty considerations.

All this my countrymen did not understand, and I did not choose to make them my father-confessors. So they excommunicated me. All were against me.

The fact that all were against me — that there was no longer any one outside my own family circle of whom I could say: 'He believes in me' — must, as you can easily see, have aroused a mood which found its outlet in *The Pretenders*. But enough on this subject.

Exactly at the time when *The Pretenders* came out, Frederick VII died, and the war began. I wrote a poem, 'En broder i nöd' (A Brother in Need). The Norwegian Americanism which had driven me back at every point, rendered it ineffectual. Then I went into exile!

About the time of my arrival at Copenhagen, the Danes were defeated at Dybböl. In Berlin I saw King William's triumphal entry with trophies and booty. During those days *Brand* began to grow within me like an embryo. When I arrived in Italy, the work of unification there had already been completed by means of a spirit of self-sacrifice which knew no bounds. Add to this, Rome with its ideal peace, association with the care-free artist community, an existence in an atmosphere which can be compared only with that of Shakespeare's *As You Like It* — and you have the conditions productive of *Brand*. It is a great mistake to suppose that I have depicted the life and career of Sören Kierkegaard. (I have read very little of S. K., and understood even less.) That Brand is a clergyman is really immaterial; the demand, 'All or nothing,' is made in all domains of life — in love, in art, etc. Brand is myself in my best moments — just as certainly as it is certain that by self-analysis I brought to light many of both Peer Gynt's and Stensgaard's qualities.

AUGUST STRINDBERG

THE LAST ACT

The final act is the most important one in a drama, and a dramatist generally begins his work at the end. We sit out a long evening at the theatre in order to see the last act or 'how it will go.' But in the significant lives of certain men people like to ignore the last act, because it is uncomfortable and might show how the godless fare at last. He who wrote the operetta *Boccaccio* had to append the last act to it; the jovial Florentine became a priest and delivered lectures on Dante's *Hell*, though he only reached the seventeenth canto. Voltaire's last hours, when he took the sacrament, might furnish a subject for a tragedy like the second part of Faust. Heine announced his conversion, which took place in 1851, in the preface to the *Romancero*: 'I have returned to God like the prodigal son, after I had fed swine with the Hegelians for a long time.' This preface should be printed before every collection of Heine's poems. Hegel singing penitential psalms on his death-bed might form the subject of a fresco painting for the entrance-hall of Berlin University. But the most affecting final act is Oscar Wilde's description of his prison life in *De Profundis*. He was the so-called renaissance leader, who disinterred heathenism with its false worship of beauty, which contains the foulest of all. Kierkegaard would have called him the æsthete, the Sybarite cold as cast iron, the egoist round whose petty 'I' the whole world was to revolve in order to understand him alone. Many, led astray like him by the seducing spirits of his youth, remained fairly free from public punishment. Wilde seems to have been picked out to furnish a startling example, for his position, at any rate in his own country, was almost that of an idol.

What he wrote lacks originality; it is whipped-up foam; glazing which, when washed off, leaves no texture; it is as restless as cross-lights, or like a mirror in a public restaurant, in a labyrinthine hall with deceptive lines and false perspectives; it runs out of the hand like albumen or frog-spawn; it is perverse as in *Dorian Grey*, the hero of which should have lost his youth by nightly excesses, while on the contrary it is only his portrait which changes.

The last act was played, and that outdid all horror, was so horrible that Wilde himself could not describe its details, which, however, oral tradition has preserved in a Swedenborgian legend.

De Profundis arouses pity and fear, and one would gladly acquit the man who was perhaps the victim of his delusion; a worldly tribunal would not have judged him if he had not himself appealed to it, and that indeed for a wrong done him. It was what our renaissance-critic called a 'piece of stupidity' when he made Wilde out to be a martyr of 'hypocrisy,' as he called justice. Wilde however seems to have taken another view of the matter to his impartial defender: 'A day in prison on which one does not weep is a day on which one's heart is hard, not a day on which one's heart is happy. Once I had put into motion the forces of society, society turned on me and said: "Have you been living all this time in defiance of my laws, and do you now appeal to those laws for protection? You shall have those laws exercised to the full." A man's very highest moment, I have no doubt at all, is when he kneels in the dust and beats his breast and tells us all the sins of his life.'

The 'joy of life' whose perfume he had inhaled at Oxford through Pater's *Renaissance* now began to grow sour.

'Clergymen and people who use phrases without wisdom sometimes talk of suffering as a mystery. It is really a revelation.

'Behind joy and laughter there may be a temperament coarse, hard, and callous. Pain, unlike pleasure, wears no mask. There are times when sorrow seems to me to be the only truth. The secret of life is suffering.'

Let us add that Wilde derived his most dangerous doctrine from Baudelaire and Shakespeare's sonnets. And let us close with the new view of the Renaissance which he attained to in prison: 'To me one of the things in history the most to be regretted is that the Christ's own renaissance, which has produced the Cathedral at Chartres, the Arthurian cycle of legends, the life of St. Francis of Assisi, the art of Giotto, and Dante's Divine Comedy, was not allowed to develop on its own lines, but was interrupted and spoiled by the dreary classical Renaissance.'

RUSSIAN WRITERS
FYODOR MICHAILOVITCH DOSTOEVSKY

One thing is a pity: he (Pissemsky) writes too fast. He writes much too fast, and much too much. A man should have more ambition, more respect for his talent and his craft, and more love for art. When one's young, ideas come crowding incredibly into one's head; but one should not capture each and all of them as it flies, and rush to give it forth. One should rather await the synthesis, and think more; wait till the many single details which make up an idea have gathered themselves into a nucleus, into a large, imposing picture; then, and not till then, should one write them down. The colossal figures, created by the colossal writers, have often grown out of long, stubborn labour.

You said once, brother, that I had not read Schiller. You are mistaken. I have him by heart, I have spoken his speech and dreamed his dreams; and I believe that it was a peculiarly good stroke of luck that made me acquainted with the great poet in that special period of my life. I could never have learnt to know Schiller so well as precisely in those days.

But I have vowed to myself that, however hard it

may go with me, I'll pull myself together, and in no circumstances will I work to order. Work done to order would oppress and blight me. I want each of my efforts to be incontrovertibly good. Just look at Pushkin and Gogol. Both wrote very little, yet both have deserved national memorials. Gogol now gets a thousand roubles a printed page, while Pushkin had, as you know well, as much as a ducat a line of verse. Both — but particularly Gogol — bought their fame at the price of years of dire poverty.

Perhaps it will interest you to know what I do when I'm not writing — well, I read. I read a great deal, and it has a curious effect on me. When I re-read anything that I knew years ago, I feel fresh powers in myself. I can pierce to the heart of the book, grasp it entire, and from it draw new confidence in myself.

My novel, which I simply can't break loose from, keeps me endlessly at work. If I had known beforehand how it would be, I should never have begun it at all. I decided to do it all over again, and, by God! that has improved it a lot. Now I'm ready with it once more, and this revision is really the last. I have given myself my word not to touch it again. After all, it's the fate of all first books to be altered over and over again. I don't know whether Chateaubriand's 'Atala' was his first book, but I do know that he re-wrote it seventeen times. Pushkin did just the same with quite short poems. Gogol used to polish away at his wonderful works for two years at a time, and if you have read the 'Sentimental Journey,' that witty book by Sterne, you'll very likely remember what Walter Scott, in his article on Sterne, says with reference to Sterne's servant, La Fleur. La Fleur declared that his master had filled about two hundred quires of paper with the description of his journey through France. Now, the question is, What became of all that paper? The result was a little book, for writing which a parsimonious person (such as, for example, Plyushkin) would have used half a quire.

Everybody looks upon me as a wonder of the world. If I but open my mouth, the air resounds with what Dostoevsky said, what Dostoevsky means to do. Bielinski loves me unboundedly. The writer Turgeniev, who has just returned from Paris, has from the first been more than friendly; and Bielinski declares that Turgeniev has quite lost his heart to me. T. is a really splendid person! I've almost lost my own heart to *him*. A highly gifted writer, an aristocrat, handsome, rich, intelligent, cultured, and only twenty-five — I really don't know what more he could ask from fate. Besides all that, he has an unusually upright, fine, well-disciplined nature. Do read his story, 'Andrey Kolossov,' in the *Otetchestvennia Zapiski*. The hero is himself, though he did not intend to depict his own character.

As for myself, I was for some time utterly discouraged. I have one terrible vice: I am unpardonably ambitious and egotistic. The thought that I had disappointed all the hopes set on me, and spoilt what might have been a really significant piece of work, depressed me very heavily. The thought of 'Goliadkin' made me sick. I wrote a lot of it too quickly, and in moments of fatigue. The first half is better than the second. Alongside many brilliant passages are others so disgustingly bad that I can't read them myself.

NIKOLAI VASILIEVITCH GOGOL

Thankless is the task of the writer who dares reproduce what is constantly passing before the eyes of all, unnoticed by our distracted gaze: all the disgusting little annoyances and trials of our every-day lives; the ordinary, indifferent characters we must constantly meet and put up with. How they hinder and weary us! Such a writer will not have the applause of the masses; contemporary critics will consider his creations both low and useless, and will assign him an inferior place among those writers who scoff at humanity. He will be declared wanting in heart, soul, and talent. For his critic will not admit those instruments to be equally marvelous, one of which reveals the sun and the other the motions of invisible animalculae; neither will he admit what depth of thought is required to make a masterpiece of a picture, the subject of which is drawn from the darker side of human life....

Those who have analyzed my powers as a writer have not discerned the important element of my nature, or my peculiar bent. Pushkin alone perceived it. He always said that I was especially endowed to bring into relief the trivialities of life, to analyze an ordinary character, to bring to light the little peculiarities which escape general observation. This is, I think, my strong point. The reader resents the baseness of my heroes; after reading the book he returns joyfully to the light of day. I should have been pardoned had I only created picturesque villains; their baseness is what will never be pardoned. A Russian shrinks before the picture of his nothingness.

The cause of that gaiety which one had noticed in my first works was a kind of inner need. I became a prey to fits of melancholy which were beyond my comprehension.... In order to get rid of them I invented the funniest things I could think of. I invented funny characters in the funniest situations imaginable.

I never created anything out of mere imagination. Only in those things was I successful which I took from reality and which were based on the data I knew. I could fathom a man then only when I had seen all the minutest details of his exterior. Yet I never *painted* a portrait by simply copying it. I *created* portraits, but I created them on that of mere imagination. The more details I had seen and considered, the better were my productions. My mind is in this respect thoroughly Russian, that is, a mind capable of deriving rather than of inventing.

I saw that in my former works I laughed for nothing, uselessly, without knowing why. If it is necessary to laugh, then let us laugh at that which really deserves to be laughed at by all. In my *Revizor* I decided to gather in one place and deride all that is bad in Russia, all the evils which are being perpetrated in those places where the utmost rectitude is required from man.

A contemporary author who writes comedies and describes manners must be as far from his own country as possible. No prophet can earn glory in his own fatherland. I don't mind the fact that all classes of society have risen against me; yet it is somewhat sad and depressing to see my own countrymen, whom I sincerely love, attack me with no justice, to see in what a perverted way they accept and interpret everything.

None of my readers knows that in laughing at my characters they laughed at myself. In me there was a collection of all possible defects and in a greater quantity than in any other man.... If they had suddenly and all together appeared before my eyes I would have hanged myself.... I began to depict in my heroes my own nastiness. This is how I did it. Having taken some bad feature of mine or other, I persecuted it under a different name and in a different rôle, endeavouring to make it appear before my eyes as my deadly enemy — an enemy who had inflicted a terrible injury upon me; I persecuted it with malice, with irony, with anything I could get hold of. Had any one seen those monsters which came from under my pen at the beginning, he would have shivered with fear.

ALEXANDER PUSHKIN

Yield thee not, poet, to the popular cry;
Full soon doth perish the world's noisy praise;
The fool's contempt, the cold crowd's sneer, thine eye
Doth surely mark. Be thou then firm, and gaze
Unmoved. Thou'rt king. In thy calm royalty
Go freely 'mid thy solitary ways,
Whose genius shall bear fruit in future days,
And ask not meed for actions great and high.
In *thee* is thy reward. Thou art the spirit
Of Judgment's self — best critic of true merit.

Doth this content thy soul, O Craftsmen holy?
Then let the mob come on, thy genius spurning,
Spit on the altars where thy fire is burning,
And shake thy tripod in their childish folly.

I imitated Shakespeare in his broad and free delineation of character. I followed Karamzin in his bright development of incident, and I endeavored to comprehend the form of thought and the style of language of those days. The sources are rich, very rich. Whether I succeeded in making the best of them, I do not know.... But I confess openly, the failure of my drama would distress me, because I am convinced that our theatre should proceed in accordance with the laws of the Shakesperian drama and not in the wordly fashion of Racine.

LEO TOLSTOI

April 7th, 8 A.M. 1847. — Until recently I never kept a diary, for I never could see the use of one; but, now, that I am developing my faculties, a diary will help me to judge of that development's progress. Hence the diary must contain a table of rules. Also, it must define my future activities.

For the 29th. From 5 to 10, write; from 10 to 2,

business matters; from 2 to 4, gymnastics; from 4 to 6, dinner; from 6 to 8, writing; from 8 to 10, Volkonski.

March 29th. — In my writing showed *sloth and haste;* in my business affairs *absence of mind;* in my gymnastics *faintheartedness*. Dined, did no writing at all, and visited Volkonski and Kulikovski; was minded to *play at little*.

Hope is bad for the happy man, and good for the unhappy. I have gained much since the day when first I began to occupy myself. Yet I am greatly dissatisfied, for the further one goes in the task of perfecting oneself, the more faults are detected. Well has Socrates said that the supreme stage in man's perfection is knowledge that there is nothing of which he has knowledge.

A writer is dear and necessary for us only in the measure in which he reveals to us the inner working of his soul, of course, if this work is new, and not previously accomplished. No matter what he may write, a drama, a learned work, a story, a philosophic treatise, a lyric poem, a criticism, a satire, it is only this inner work of his soul which is dear to us, and not the architectural structure in which he, for the most part, and I think, always, distorting them, clothes his thoughts and feelings.

I have long ago formed a rule to judge every artistic production from three sides: (1) from the side of its contents, — in how far that which is revealed by the artist from a new side is important and necessary for men, because every production is a production of art only when it reveals a new side of life; (2) to what extent the form of the production is good, beautiful, and in correspondence with the contents; and (3) in how far the relation of the artist to his subject is sincere, that is, in how far he believes in what he represents. This last quality always seems to me to be the most important one in an artistic production. It gives to an artistic production its force, makes an artistic production infectious, that is evokes in the hearer and reader those sensations which the artist experiences.

Thus, if a man considers his life to be his, and its end to be the worldly good, for himself or for other men, this life can have for him no rational meaning. Life receives a rational meaning only when a man understands that the recognition of his life as his own, and the good of personality, of his own or that of others, as its end, is an error, and that the human life does not belong to him, who has received this life from some one, but to Him who produced this life, and so its end must not consist in the attainment of his own good or of the good of others, but only in the fulfilment of the will of Him who produced it. Only with such a comprehension of life does it receive a rational meaning, and its end, which consists in the fulfilment of God's will, become attainable, and, above all, only with such a comprehension does man's activity become clearly defined, and he no longer is subject to despair and suffering, which were inevitable with his former comprehension.

Now it is summer, and, as usual, life fills me with transport and I forget to work. This year I have struggled for a long time, but the beauty of the world has conquered me.

IVAN TURGENIEV

I feel in the vein for work, and this notwithstanding that I have left the enthusiasm of youth far behind me. I write with a calmness which astonishes me. Let us hope that the work will not suffer therefrom. Coldness generally implies mediocrity.

You [Flaubert] must not forget, moreover, that men are measured according to the measure they have given of themselves, and you are bearing the burden of your past.

My publisher keeps circling round me like an eagle, screaming for *something*.

Madame Sand's death has been a great, great grief to me.... There was no public upon which Madame Sand had more influence than the Russian public, and of course I ought to have said so!... What a heart of gold she had! What an entire absence there was in her of anything small, mean, or false. What a good fellow she was, and what a delightful woman!

Well, now I am going to astonish you! Never in my life have I worked as I've been working here. I spend sleepless nights, bent double over my writing-table. I'm once more filled with the illusion that I can say, not exactly something different from what has ever been said before — that I don't care about — but that I can say it differently.

Thank you for having made me read Tolstoi's novel (*La Guerre et la Paix*). It belongs to the very first rank. What a word-painter and what a psychologist! The two first volumes are *sublime*, but the third goes off terribly. He repeats himself, and he philosophises! In a word, one realises the man himself, the author and the Russian, while till then one had realised nothing but nature and humanity. Occasionally it seems to me there are things worthy of Shakespeare. I kept uttering cries of admiration as I read it,... and it's long. Yes, it's great, really great.

Oh, this literature that smells of the lamp! The principal quality of Tolstoi's work is precisely that it breathes of life itself.

I am working here like a galley-slave. I go up to bed at 2 o'clock, and to sleep at 3. I get up at 9 in the daytime.

At all events, if you want to publish a series of articles in the *Gaulois* upon great foreign writers — an idea which meets with my entire approbation, and for which I put myself entirely at your disposal in the matter of getting information, etc. — I must beg you to let me take my proper place and pass in my proper turn.

Begin, for instance, in the case of Russia, by Pushkin and Gogol; in that of England, by Dickens; in that of Germany, by Goethe, at whom Barbey d'Aurevilly has stupidly been throwing mud just lately; and then, if you find it takes, you can pass on to the *dii minorum gentium*.

I cannot disguise from you, however, that on principle and as a general rule I am against any sort of adaptation of novels for the stage, and especially in this particular case, *Roudine* being a psychological study.

SOURCES OF QUOTATIONS

The following list of sources from which quotations have been chosen for this volume is appended with the belief that many readers will find a wealth of further ideas in the works herein suggested. The editors have been particularly fortunate in having access to the unusual collection in the Widener Library of Harvard University, a privilege for which they wish to express appreciation.

AMERICAN WRITERS

Beecher as a Humorist. Selections from the published works of Henry Ward Beecher. Compiled by Eleanor Kirk. New York: Fords, Howard & Hulbert, 1887.

The Heart of Burroughs's Journals. Edited by Clara Barrus. Boston: Houghton Mifflin Company, 1928.

The Life and Letters of Emily Dickinson. By her niece, Martha Dickinson Bianchi. Boston: Houghton Mifflin Company, 1924.

Letters and Social Aims. By Ralph Waldo Emerson. Boston: Houghton Mifflin Company.

Journals of Ralph Waldo Emerson. Edited by Edward Waldo Emerson and Waldo Emerson Forbes. Vol. X. Boston: Houghton Mifflin Company, 1914.

The Beauties of Franklin. Selections from his works. By Alfred Howard. London: Thomas Tegg.

The Heart of Hawthorne's Journals. Edited by Newton Arvin. Boston: Houghton Mifflin Company, 1929.

Hawthorne. By Newton Arvin. Boston: Little, Brown & Co., 1929.

Postscripts. By O. Henry. New York: Harper & Bros., 1923.

O. Henry. A Biography by C. Alphonso Smith. New York: Doubleday, 1916.

The Autocrat of the Breakfast Table. By Oliver Wendell Holmes. Boston: Houghton Mifflin Company.

Literature and Life. By William Dean Howells. New York: Harper & Bros., 1902.

Readings from Washington Irving. Selected from *The Sketch-Book* and *The Alhambra.* New York: G. P. Putnam's Sons, 1888.

The Letters of William James. Edited by his son, Henry James. Boston: Atlantic Monthly Press, 1920.

SOURCES OF QUOTATIONS

Life of Henry Wadsworth Longfellow. Edited by Samuel Longfellow. Boston: Ticknor & Co., 1886.
The Complete Works of James Russell Lowell. Boston: Houghton Mifflin Company.
Letters of James Whitcomb Riley. Edited by William Lyon Phelps. Indianapolis: Bobbs-Merrill Company, 1930.
Autumn, from the Journal of Henry D. Thoreau. Edited by H. G. O. Blake. Boston: Houghton Mifflin Company, 1892.
Familiar Letters of Henry David Thoreau. Edited by F. B. Sanborn. Boston: Houghton Mifflin Company, 1894.
Mark Twain's Autobiography. An Introduction by Albert Bigelow Paine. New York: Harper & Bros., 1924.
Two Prefaces. By Walt Whitman. New York: Doubleday, Page, & Co., 1926.

BRITISH WRITERS

Selections from Addison and Steele. Edited by Will D. Howe. New York: Charles Scribner's Sons, 1921.
Poetry and Prose of William Blake. Edited by Geoffrey Keynes. London: Nonesuch Press, 1927.
Boswell's Life of Johnson. Edited by Charles Grosvenor Osgood. New York: Charles Scribner's Sons, 1917.
The Brontës, Life and Letters. By Clement Shorter. London: Hodder & Stoughton, 1908.
The Complete Works of Elizabeth Barrett Browning. Edited by Charlotte Porter and Helen A. Clarke. New York: T. Y. Crowell & Co., 1900.
Letters of Robert Burns. Edited by Francis H. Allen. Boston: Houghton Mifflin Company.
Samuel Butler: Characters and Passages from Note-Books. Edited by A. R. Waller. Cambridge (England): University Press, 1908.
The Confessions of Lord Byron. Arranged by W. A. Lewis Bettany. London: John Murray, 1905.
Life of Lord Byron: With His Letters and Journals. By Thomas Moore. Boston: Little, Brown & Co.
Anthology of Prose. Samuel Taylor Coleridge. By S. L. Edwards. New York: E. P. Dutton & Co.
Letters from Joseph Conrad. Edited by Edward Garnett. Indianapolis: Bobbs-Merrill Company, 1928.
Letters of Charles Dickens. New York: Charles Scribner's Sons, 1889.

SOURCES OF QUOTATIONS

Wit and Wisdom of Benjamin Disraeli. By H. G. Halcraft. New York: D. Appleton & Co., 1881.
The Later Years of Thomas Hardy. By Florence Emily Hardy. New York: Macmillan Company, 1930.
Essays by William Hazlitt. Edited by Percy Van Dyke Shelly. New York: Charles Scribner's Sons, 1924.
The Dramatic Works of William Shakespeare. Preface by Dr. Samuel Johnson. London: Carpenter & Son.
Nineteenth Century Letters: John Keats. By Byron J. Reese. New York: Charles Scribner's Sons.
Critical Essays. By Charles Lamb. New York: Dutton, 1903.
An Essay on Comedy. By George Meredith. Edited by Lane Cooper. New York: Charles Scribner's Sons, 1918.
The Prose Works of John Milton. London: Henry G. Bohn, 1848.
Representative Essays on the Theory of Style. Chosen by William T. Brewster. New York: Macmillan Company, 1905.
Style. By Walter Raleigh. London: Edward Arnold, 1897.
The True and the Beautiful in Nature, Art, Morals, and Religion. Selected from the Works of John Ruskin. New York: John Wiley, 1878.
The Journal of Sir Walter Scott. From the Original Manuscript at Abbotsford. Edinburgh: David Douglas, 1890.
Letters and Recollections of Sir Walter Scott. Edited by Horace G. Hutchinson. London: Smith, Elder & Co., 1904.
The Life and Correspondence of the Late Robert Southey. Edited by his son, Charles Cuthbert Southey. London: Longmans, 1850.
The Works of Robert Louis Stevenson. London: T. & A. Constable, 1897.
Essays of Travel and in the Art of Writing. By Robert Louis Stevenson. New York: Charles Scribner's Sons, 1923.
Extracts from the Writings of William M. Thackeray. London: Smith, Elder & Co., 1881.

THE CLASSICS

Aristotle's Theory of Poetry and Fine Art. By S. H. Butcher. New York: Macmillan Company, 1902.
Demetrius on Style. Translated by W. Rhys Roberts. Cambridge (England): University Press, 1902.
Plato the Teacher. Edited by William Lowe Bryan. New York: Charles Scribner's Sons, 1879.

SOURCES OF QUOTATIONS

FRENCH WRITERS

Honoré de Balzac. Letters to Madame Hanska. Translated by Katharine Prescott Wormeley. Boston: Little, Brown & Co., 1901.
The Memoirs of François René Vicomte de Chateaubriand. Translated by Alexander Teixeira de Mattos. London: Freemantle, 1902.
Recollections of Italy, England, and America. By F. R. de Chateaubriand. Philadelphia: M. Carey, 1816.
Diderot's Thoughts on Art and Style. Translated by Beatrix L. Tollemache. London: Remington, 1893.
The Memoirs of Alexandre Dumas (Père). Translated by A. F. Davidson. London: Allen, 1891.
Sketches and Reviews. (Quotation from Flaubert.) By Walter Pater. New York: Boni & Liveright, 1919.
Anatole France Himself: A Boswellian Record. By His Secretary, Jean Jacques Brousson. Translated by John Pollock. Philadelphia: J. B. Lippincott Company, 1925.
Anatole France—Representative Stories. By George Neely Henning. Boston: D. C. Heath & Co., 1924.
William Shakespeare. By Victor Hugo. London: Hurst & Blackett, 1864.
Rarahu, or the Marriage of Loti. By Pierre Loti. Translated by Clara Bell. New York: Gottsberger, 1890.
Molière. Translated by Katharine Prescott Wormeley. Boston: Little, Brown & Co., 1917.
Essays of Montaigne. Translated by George B. Ives. Cambridge: Harvard University Press, 1925.
Letters from Racine the Elder to His Son. London: T. Wilkins, 1785.
The Confessions of Jean-Jacques Rousseau. By Ed. Hédouin. Edinburgh: Oliver & Boyd, 1904.
Essays by Sainte-Beuve. London: Walter Scott.
Letters of George Sand. Translated by Veronica Lucas. Boston: Houghton Mifflin Company, 1930.
Voltaire in His Letters. By S. G. Tallentyre. New York: G. P. Putnam's Sons, 1919.

GERMAN WRITERS

Correspondence between Goethe and Carlyle. Edited by Charles Eliot Norton. New York: Macmillan Company, 1887.

SOURCES OF QUOTATIONS

Heinrich Heine's Memoirs. Edited by Gustav Karpeles. Translated by Gilbert Cannan. London: William Heinemann, 1910.
Laocoön. By Gotthold Ephraim Lessing. Translated by Ellen Frothingham. Boston: Roberts Bros., 1877.
The Complete Works of Friedrich Nietzsche. Edited by Oscar Levy. Edinburgh: T. N. Foulis, 1909.
The Æsthetic Letters, Essays, and the Philosophical Letters of Schiller. Translated by J. Weiss. Boston: Little, Brown & Co., 1845.
The Essays of Arthur Schopenhauer. Translated by T. Bailey Saunders. London: Swan Sonnenschein, 1891.

SCANDINAVIAN WRITERS

Eminent Authors of the Nineteenth Century. By Georg Brandes. Translated by Rasmus B. Anderson. New York: T. Y. Crowell & Co., 1886.
Letters of Henrik Ibsen. Translated by John Nilsen Laurvik and Mary Morison Fox. New York: Duffield & Co., 1905.
Zones of the Spirit: A Book of Thoughts. By August Strindberg. London: George Allen, 1913.

RUSSIAN WRITERS

Letters of Fyodor Michailovitch Dostoevsky. Translated by Ethel Colburn Mayne. London: Chatto & Windus, 1914.
The Russian Novelists. Translated by Jane Loring Edmands. Boston: D. Lothrop & Co., 1898.
Gogol. By Janko Lavrin. New York: E. P. Dutton & Co., 1926.
The Diaries of Leo Tolstoy. Translated by C. J. Hogarth and A. Sirnis. New York: E. P. Dutton & Co., 1917.
The Kingdom of God is Within You. By Leo Tolstoi. Translated by Leo Wiener. London: J. M. Dent & Sons.
Turgeniev, and His French Circle. Edited by E. Halperine-Kaminsky. Translated by Ethel M. Arnold. London: T. Fisher Unwin, 1898.